In the Steps of
the Great American Herpetologist

Karl
Patterson
Schmidt

In the Steps of
the Great American Herpetologist

Karl Patterson Schmidt

)ঝ

by A. Gilbert Wright

Illustrations by Matthew Kalmenoff

)ঝ

Published by
M. Evans and Company, Inc., New York
and distributed in association with
J. B. Lippincott Company,
Philadelphia and New York

M Evans
Lanham • New York • Boulder • Toronto • Plymouth, UK

M. Evans
An imprint of The Rowman & Littlefield Publishing Group, Inc.
4501 Forbes Boulevard, Suite 200, Lanham, Maryland 20706
http://www.rlpgtrade.com

10 Thornbury Road, Plymouth PL6 7PP, United Kingdom

Distributed by National Book Network

British Library Cataloguing in Publication Information Available

Library of Congress Cataloging-in-Publication Data Available

ISBN 13: 978-1-59077-360-4 (pbk: alk. paper)

♾™ The paper used in this publication meets the minimum requirements of
American National Standard for Information Sciences—Permanence of Paper for
Printed Library Materials, ANSI/NISO Z39.48-1992.

Printed in the United States of America

Designed by Robin Sherwood

Contents

ACKNOWLEDGMENTS

This story of Karl Schidt's life could not have been written without the generous help of Karl's widow, Margaret Wightman Schmidt, his sister, Margaret S. Bergseng, his brother, John R. Schmidt, and his two sons, John M. Schnidt and Robert G. Schmidt. They provided me with a wealth of information, and with many of Karl's letters. Many letters and other papers relating to Karl's career were loaned to me by the Field Museum of Natural History, through Dr. Robert F. Inger, Curator of Reptiles, and the American Museum of Natural History, through Mr. Charles M. Bogert, Chairman of the Department of Herpetology.

I am indebted to Robert Inger, as well as to Doris M. Cochran and James A. Peters of the Smithsonian Institution for reading my typescript and offereing numerous suggestions for its improvement. I would like to thank John Malone for his part in making the book a better one. And I would like to thank my wife, Lydia Kirchherr Wright, for her many helpful suggestions and for her patience.

A. Gilbert Wright

1
Karl's Formative Years

It wasn't really surprising that Karl Patterson Schmidt grew up to be a natural scientist. He came from a family whose interests were about equally divided between the natural and the academic worlds. Karl's mother, Margaret Patterson Schmidt, who had been born about fifty miles west of Chicago, near Plainfield, attended nearby North Central College. Among other college courses, she studied botany and astronomy, subjects which she would begin to teach Karl something about even when he was a very small boy. It was at college, too, that Margaret Patterson met and later married a young man from southern Minnesota, a student of foreign languages and an ardent outdoorsman named George Washington Schmidt. Soon after graduation and marriage, Karl's father became professor of German language and literature at Lake

Forest College in Lake Forest, Illinois. It was here, in this suburban town lying along the shore of Lake Michigan just north of Chicago, that Karl was born on June 19, 1890.

"Tell me, Karl," his mother asked one day when he was four years old, "what kind of tree is that?"

"A red oak, Mother," the boy replied.

His mother had taught him to recognize the chestnut tree, too, as well as the trillium and the wild larkspur. At night, when the trees were only rustling shadows, difficult to tell apart, his mother identified the stars for him instead, so that he knew the constellations of Cygnus, Lyra, and Orion, and could pick out from among all those high flickering lights the steady glow of the more conspicuous planets, Mars and Venus and Jupiter.

At the same time that his mother was introducing Karl to the natural world, his father was teaching him to read and to speak German as well as English. Karl was to learn a lot more German very soon, for, when he was five years old, his parents left Lake Forest for a year of graduate study in Europe. Karl's father attended the University of Freiberg, in southwest Germany, and during his vacations took his wife and son on short excursions to England, Holland, and Switzerland. The only trouble about all the German that Professor Schmidt had taught his son was that Karl sometimes got mixed up and used German grammar when he was speaking English. But once the family was back in Lake Forest, Karl's English grammar rapidly improved.

As his schooling progressed, Karl found that he

was most interested in geography and history—perhaps because of the travelling in foreign countries he had done with his parents. It was the legendary heroes of history who first captured his imagination—King Arthur, Robin Hood, and William Tell, for instance—heroes whom he himself could pretend to be when playing after school in the hills and ravines and along the sandy beaches of his home town. But as he grew older, he spent less time reliving the adventures of his favorite heroes, and more time reading about new places and people, taking out every history book he could find in the school library.

There was another stimulus to these interests of Karl's, too. Lake Forest was less than an hour by direct train to Chicago; and Chicago at the turn of the century had developed into one of the most interesting cities in the country. When Karl had been only three years old, in 1893, the "Chicago World's Fair" had opened, the great Columbian Exposition celebrating the 400th anniversary of the discovery of America. By 1900, when Karl was ten, the only actual structure remaining from the great fair in Jackson Park was the Palace of Art, but it had been regarded as the most beautiful of all the World's Fair buildings. What was more, the Palace of Art housed the extraordinary Field Columbian Museum, a kind of anthology of all the most valuable and important of the exhibits shown at the fair seven years before, including everything from precious stones to a collection of mounted birds, mammals, and other natural history specimens from all over the world.

But the Field Columbian Museum was only one of many places to visit in Chicago, though it may have been the most spectacular. Lying on the grass in some shady spot in Jackson Park, eating a picnic lunch with his family on a bright Sunday in spring, Karl felt the world to be very full, packed with things to be seen and learned about.

"I wish I hadn't been so small when we went to Germany," said Karl suddenly. "I mean, l love Chicago, but I want to see every city and museum in the world."

His mother smiled at him. "Perhaps you will," she said.

But his father added, "There are more than just cities to see, you know, Karl. I think it's time you learned about living out of doors, in the woods. That can be as interesting as any museum." He paused for a moment, and then asked, "How would you like to go with me on a camping trip this summer—to Wisconsin?"

"Do you really mean it?" Karl replied.

"Yes, I do mean it, son," his father said.

And so that summer found father and son camped beside one of a chain of lakes in northern Wisconsin, with their tent pitched on a rise of ground close to a cooling spring. They were twenty miles from the nearest town, but a trail connecting the chain of lakes led close by them, and from time to time Indians and other campers would pass their way, stopping for a drink of water or to ask about the fishing. The boy and his father were there for seven weeks in that summer of 1900. Karl learned to swim and to fish, to feel at home in a canoe, and to go all day with nothing to eat but jerked venison—long strips of deer meat that had been dried in the sun. Behind the lake virgin forests hemmed the campers in. The cathedral silence and the solitude of those woods filled Karl with awe. Sometimes they even frightened him. For he was as yet only ten—who could tell what lay in the deep shadows between the high trees, where there was no sun?

One afternoon, without telling his father what he was going to do, Karl jumped into a rowboat which some campers had tied to shore beside their camp, and pushed out into the lake. Unaccustomed to rowing alone, he lifted the oars out of their sockets —and watched in guilty dismay as one of the oar-locks slipped down the oar and fell with a splash into ten feet of water. At that moment, his father appeared on shore and discovered what had happened. He told Karl how to paddle back to shore by using a single oar, first on one side of the boat and then on the other, as though he were in a canoe. As Professor Schmidt tied up the boat again, he said, "You'll have to replace that oarlock, Karl."

It would be possible to get another one at the head of the trail, a half-mile hike through forest and swamp—and his father insisted that Karl should go alone.

Hoping that his father would call him back, or join him, Karl started out very slowly, yelling at the top of his voice to give himself courage. But all too soon he found himself over the crest of a hill a hundred yards or so from camp, and his father was out of sight. Karl began to run downhill toward the swamp. The silence of the woods frightened him, and his own imagination frightened him even more. Passing a small clearing in the woods where he and his father had picked raspberries a few days earlier, he remembered that they had seen a number of bushes which had been trampled by a bear. His heart banging against his chest, he glanced anxiously toward the bushes, and hurried on. But then, as he approached the edge of the swamp, he met the campers whose oarlock he had lost, and they told him they hadn't seen any bears at all.

A narrow "pole-trail," a kind of sidewalk composed of tamarack poles laid end to end, led across the murky swamp. Once, he fell off the pole-trail into the knee-deep sphagnum quagmire. Soaking wet, he pulled himself out of the moss and roots and went forward again. He couldn't help remembering, though, that the northern swamps were a habitat of wolves and wildcats. His heart began to bang again. After all, how could he have known that fifteen years later he would spend some of the most exciting and happiest months of his life wading through a Louisiana swamp far murkier than this one, and inhabited by real snakes instead of imaginary wildcats?

At any rate, his mission was a success: he got the new oarlock and carried it safely back to camp. He began to realize that he had had an adventure. Now that it was over it even seemed to have been fun. Perhaps there wasn't any reason to be afraid of the deep woodland shadows after all.

The woods began to be a part of Karl's life. He grew to love them as much as his father did. Eventually, when his sister and brothers became old enough to be taken along, Karl helped his father teach them the things that he had already learned.

Back at school in Lake Forest, Karl's progress was so rapid that he managed to complete all eight grades in five years, graduating at the age of twelve. Partly because he skipped so many grades, and partly because he became so absorbed with reading, he made few close friends among his classmates. Karl's after-school companions were discovered in the pages of the famous children's magazines, *The Youth's Companion* and *The St. Nicholas.* Later he read the historical novels of G. A. Henty and James Fenimore Cooper, spending the afternoons with Henty's Marco Polo and with Natty Bumpo of Cooper's *Leatherstocking Tales.* He kept up his German, too, reading books in that language from his father's library.

Karl went to high school at the Academy of Lake Forest College, where his major interest continued to be in literature until his third year, when he began to study natural science. In a spare room at home, he set up a chemistry laboratory. One afternoon, just as a large vial was overflowing, looking like bubble bath, Karl's mother came into the room.

"Mercy," she said, "I've never seen such a mess. And what's that enormous spot on the floor?"

"Oh, I spilled some acid. I'm sorry, Mother."

"Well, just don't hurt yourself. And you'd better be sure you grow up to be a genius, young man."

Karl grinned. "I'll try," he said.

His laboratory didn't distract Karl from his school work, though, and, when he graduated from Lake

Forest Academy at sixteen, he was awarded the Haven Medal as the scholastic leader of his class.

Karl entered Lake Forest College as a freshman in the fall of 1906, taking courses in mathematics, chemistry, English grammar and composition, and French. But the course that excited him most was biology, a science new to Karl, taught that year by a brilliant young naturalist named James C. Needham. James Needham not only got Karl interested in biology in the first place, but a number of years later was to play an important role in the sequence of events that brought about Karl's decision to become a herpetologist. Before that time would come, though, Karl's way of life would undergo a drastic change.

One spring evening during Karl's freshman year at college, his father sat down with him to have a long talk. Professor Schmidt wanted to move his wife and four children to a farm near the town of Stanley in Clark County, Wisconsin. He himself would continue teaching at Lake Forest College until the farm was capable of supporting the family.

"I can't do it without you, though, Karl," he said. "You'd have to manage the farm. I've talked to some of your teachers about this, and I must admit that they aren't very happy at the idea. They believe, as I do, that you're an exceptional student, and they don't like to see your scholarly career interrupted. But once the farm is well established, you'll be able to return to college. What's more, I think that on the farm you'll be able to teach yourself a great deal. Don't you agree?"

"Of course I do," said Karl. "I think it'll be very exciting."

June 19, 1907, was Karl's seventeenth birthday; it found him in Wisconsin with his father, hard at work building the frame of their new home in a clearing in the woods, two miles from Stanley. As he paused for a moment, he saw a sudden movement at the edge of the clearing. It was a snake of some sort, sliding away into the woods. "I'll have to catch one of those sometime," Karl thought. He watched it disappear into the foliage, and then he picked up his hammer and went back to work.

2
Six Years on a Wilderness Farm

Extending halfway across the State of Wisconsin was a belt of loam some fifteen miles wide known as the Colby Loamy Clay. Composed of the decayed leaf mold of centuries, this exceptionally fertile soil assured the ultimate success of the many dairy farms that were gradually replacing the wilderness in that part of the State. But the wilderness had first to be literally uprooted. Besides assisting in the construction of the Schmidt family dwelling and the other frame buildings needed for farming (barn, hen house, and tool shed, Karl took on the main responsibility for the biggest job of all—clearing the land.

First the trees had to be cut down on more than one hundred acres of the farm. Then the brush had to be cleared, and the tree stumps, with their stubborn roots, pulled out of the ground. The fallen trees themselves were sawed into firewood, or into larger logs that were hauled away to market. Even then the job was not finished, for the countless glacial boulders that had been deposited thousands of years before, when the ice cap covered half of North America, had to be removed from the newly created fields. Only then could the land be planted in clover or grains or farm grasses, or converted into pasture and meadowland. In patches, then, little by little, the forest became fields, and crops were planted.

It isn't hard to understand why Karl's teachers felt that for a sensitive 17-year-old suburbanite student to be suddenly burdened with managing a wilderness farm, a job requiring him to be lumberjack and teamster as well as dairy farmer, would probably mean the end of his scholarly career. But Karl's teachers underrated both his strength of mind and the unusual intellectual curiosity of the entire Schmidt family. Neither Karl nor any of the rest of his family required an academic atmosphere in which to grow intellectually. For the Schmidts, farming was as much an adventure in education as it was a means of livelihood. Natural history now became their passion.

Nor did Karl give up reading and studying. That first winter of 1907, he had only a single horse and two cows to care for, which left him with lots of time for the books which lined the walls of the huge living room of their new farmhouse. He even took correspondence courses, from the University of Chicago, in English composition and comparative religion. Stretched out before the great fireplace which

18

he had helped to build, he read not only the assigned books for his courses, but other volumes that he discovered in the Stanley town library: Francis Parkman's series on early American history, Sven Hedin's *Travels in Central Asia,* and a book that recounted the stories of all the great polar expeditions up to the year 1900.

But the most important part of Karl's education was of a different kind. From his early childhood he'd been given lessons in botany and astronomy by his mother, and in woodlore and fishing and camping by his father. From Professor Needham at Lake Forest College he'd learned the basic facts of biology. Now, his new life in the wilderness gave him the perfect environment in which to put all this knowledge to work, in the observation of new phenomena which in turn would increase his knowledge still further.

In Wisconsin, the Schmidts found themselves in a climate very different from that of Illinois. The winters were much longer and colder, and the summers were much hotter. Karl became very interested in observing the changes of weather in this new locality. Even in his childhood in Lake Forest he had kept a systematic record of the weather, clipping the forecast for the following day from a Chicago newspaper and pasting it in a great ledger, so that on the next day he could write beside the clipping what the weather had actually turned out to be. Now, in the Stanley area, Karl found that there was a neighborhood rivalry in recording the lowest temperature in winter and the highest in summer.

He discovered, too, that the forecasting of weather changes was necessary to successful farming.

Karl found the stark winters of Wisconsin especially dramatic. For one thing, they were full of new sounds. Lying in bed on a bitter night, he would hear in the great silence a sudden report like that of a 30-30 rifle—and would know that a giant elm had just been split by the frost. Many of the elms bore the healed scars of these frost cracks, sometimes forty feet in length. And, going out in the morning to investigate the latest crack, Karl would find himself listening to other winter sounds— packed snow creaking and squealing beneath his feet, or the runners of his sleigh—and he noted that these sounds varied in pitch with every change in temperature.

The most spectacular of all the northern phenomena of winter weather, though, for Karl, was the Aurora Borealis, the "Northern Lights." He and his brothers and sister would get thoroughly chilled standing out in the night cold watching the steady glow of the arched bands across the northern sky, or the more familiar streamers of light shooting toward the zenith. Occasionally, they would be witness to an awe-inspiring vision, when the entire night sky was aglow, with streamers reaching upward even from the south. On one such night, when Karl was making a long drive with horse and buggy, he laid back the buggy top to get a better view of the magnificent sight, even though the temperature was well below zero.

Then winter turned toward spring. While the

snow still lay white on the northern slopes, the forty acres of woods at the back of the farm burst into pink and blue with hepatica. The hepatica was followed by a whole succession of early flowers, which took advantage of the sunlight that reached the forest floor before the trees came into leaf—the white poppy-like flower with the red root and sap for which it is called bloodroot, the variegated phlox, delicate Dutchman's-breeches, jack-in-the-pulpit, squirrel corn, with its much divided leaves, and the white waxen dogtooth violet. Then, just before the leafing out of the trees, came the glorious white trilliums, hundreds of thousands of them, climaxing the annual spring flower show of the woodland forty.

"Look at this one, Karl," called out Karl's younger brother Frank.

They were searching for freaks among the farm's million trilliums. The white trillium is normally a three-petaled and three-sepaled flower, but Frank had found one of the uncommon double trilliums that look like roses. Also, there were trilliums in fours, with four leaves, four petals, and four sepals. Even more extraordinary, there were trilliums with six green sepals but no petals, and others with six white petals but no sepals. By transplanting them from the woods, Karl and Frank were able to bring together an entire garden of freaks.

As true warm weather finally came to Clark County each year, Karl and Frank would turn to another pursuit—the making of an insect collection. From Professor Needham, at Lake Forest College, Karl had obtained his first understanding of the fascination of such a collection. Now, he and his brother determined to make an insect museum of their own, with the help of W. J. Holland's *Butterfly Book* and *Moth Book*, classic works on their subjects which are in print even today, a half century later. The two books are filled with color plates, and they made it easy for the two boys to identify their specimens.

In the daytime, they chased butterflies with an insect net; at night they collected moths by "sugaring" for them, following Dr. Holland's instructions on preparing moth bait. The boys soon learned to recognize all the common species of both moths and butterflies at sight. But there were always new and more unusual species to be discovered, and occasionally there would be a real prize, a large, spectacular beauty such as a giant swallowtail butterfly. One of those cost Frank a wild chase from the cornfield near the road, over fences and through brushcovered pastures nearly to the Wolf River, a mile away, before he could capture it with his net. Darkness held prizes for them, too: giant night-flying moths such as the brown crecropia, the green luna, or the yellow polyphemus. Other night-flying moths fastened themselves to tree trunks, their dark, mottled upper wings concealing the brilliant colors of the under wings, so that they seemed a part of the tree itself. But by day the boys, searching the woodland forty, became very clever at spotting them in spite of their camouflage.

From the lower branches of those same trees, another kind of creature—the little gray and tawny screech owls—would wail mournfully at twilight.

In fact, the woodland forty resounded with bird calls of all sorts the year around. On winter nights, barred owls and great horned owls sent forth their eerie hoots. In spring, the songs of the wood thrush and the veery floated through the woods at dusk. Before a summer shower, the black-billed cuckoo would croak hoarsely from the treetops. For the Schmidt family, the study of birds became an all-season hobby.

A pair of Baltimore orioles always nested near the house; and on a beam in the barn, above the horse stalls, a phoebe regularly built its nest, interweaving its vigorous "phoebe" call with the plaintive "pe-a-wee" of a wood pewee outside. In the sturdy oaks that had been saved for shade between the house and barn, the chipping sparrow and the flycatcher would "chip" and "chebec," as if talking with each other; and from the brushy pastures there often sounded the cheerful call of the Maryland yellow-throat: "weechity-weechity-weechity."

The winter feeding shelf would bring to the farm-yard an endless parade of winter birds—chickadees, nuthatches, downy and hairy woodpeckers, and slate-colored juncos. Once a red-bellied wood-pecker, a stray from the south, stayed at the farm all winter, paying daily visits to the feeding shelf. In a bitter cold spell, Karl discovered that a little saw-whet owl had taken up residence in a chicken house, perching contentedly beside the roosting chickens.

In later years, Karl recalled that six inches of snow once had fallen on May 1, when most of the summer birds had returned from the south to their northern homes. Led by song sparrows and fox sparrows, a great flock of summer arrivals came to the Schmidts' back door, where they were treated to quantities of chicken feed. "With their crops filled," Karl would write, "they sat about in the bushes and sang in a memorable full-throated chorus as if to thank us, to defy the snow, and to express their faith that it would go." But he remembered that four days later he had hauled a load of hay to town—on a sleigh!

During those long Wisconsin winters Karl and Frank would set traps for the common fur-bearing animals, the muskrat, weasel and mink; and, like other boys in the neighborhood, obtain pocket money from the sale of the pelts. Trapping, of course, was only a part-time activity; their season's catch amounted to two or three dozen muskrats, three or four minks, perhaps a dozen black and white skunks, together with an occasional ermine, the winter form of the larger weasel.

In the Schmidt dooryard during the warmer months, chipmunks played, helping themselves to the grain thrown out for the chickens, carting it away in their grotesquely over-stuffed cheeks for winter use. But even more entertaining than the chipmunks were the flying squirrels. They were numerous on the farm, but came out from their hiding places only after darkness had begun to fall. A dozen or more gnarled old maples on a slope near the spring at the back of the farm formed a playing ground for them. At sundown, Karl would go out with other members of the family to sit quietly on the slope and watch the furry little gliders chasing one another as though they were playing tag. The Schmidts delighted in the squirrels' graceful thirty- or forty-foot glides, and listened avidly for the soft thuds that signalled their landings at the bases of the trees, after which they could be heard scurrying to the upper branches to take off on still more glides.

During his second year on the farm, Karl received a fresh stimulus toward a scientific career. His closest friend and classmate from Lake Forest, Bernhard Dawson, who years later would become a noted astronomer, came to spend a year living with the Schmidts, and together the two boys made a number of experiments. For one thing, Bernhard had brought with him an astronomical telescope. He had purchased it on a street corner in Detroit, using all the money he had left over after buying his ticket to Wisconsin. It turned out to be an unusu- ally fine instrument, and enabled the two friends to make a serious study of astronomy, and to teach the rudiments of the subject to neighboring friends.

This interest in astronomy led to a related expe- riment. Using an old milk can full of iron, sus- pended by a long wire from the hay rack of the barn, forty feet above the driveway, Karl and Bernhard made a Foucault pendulum, demonstrat- ing to the interested neighbors who came to see it that the earth did indeed rotate on its axis. The wire was attached at the top in such a way that it was not pulled out of plumb in any direction; and, when the milk can was set swinging along a straight line drawn on the ground, it could be observed that the direction of the swing gradually changed in relation to the line below. Karl and Bernhard explained that the earth could thus be seen to revolve on its axis below the pendulum, since the pendulum's direction—its plane of oscillation—remained the same. They even showed how the line on the ground rotated a certain number of degrees each hour in relation to the pendulum's direction.

Bernhard, who was an amateur meteorologist, then turned his hand to making a properly slatted thermometer shelter, so that maximum and minimum temperatures could be read with accuracy. He also installed an intricate electric wind-direction indicator in the living room, making it unnecessary to run outdoors to see if the wind had changed.

The two companions' most unusual project was a nine-foot-long meteorological box kite. This was flown on a mile-long "string" of piano wire, reeled out from a specially constructed winch. It was long before the day when airplanes were common in the sky, and the sight of the giant kite flying overhead would cause flocks of barnyard chickens to hide all day in the brush piles, and horses of the neighborhood to run frantically through the fences of their pastures.

Following the year of Bernhard's visit, Karl spent four more years on the farm, making six years in all. He was there from the summer he turned 17 until the autumn after he became 23. Sharing vigorously and happily in all the strenuous work required in making the farm a success, he also gave his two younger brothers, Frank and John, and his sister Margaret constant help and encouragement with their school work. As his mother was often ill, he even assisted with the housework, and learned to be an expert cook.

It wasn't all work, of course. There were, for instance, neighborhood dances. Karl later decribed these outings in an essay.

"As a matter of course," he wrote, "the completion of a house or barn is celebrated by a dance, and when there is a sufficiently large threshing-floor, the whole countryside gathers for a party that is continued until dawn. When such occasions are too infrequent, the more energetic of the young men in a self-appointed committee of two or three, often arrange such barn dances any season when the weather permits and a floor is available.

"The 'committee' spreads the report that there is to be a dance, hires the music, and is responsible for what semblance of order is maintained.

"The music and beer, for such is usually supplied, are paid for by passing the hat to the male dancers. The female contingent is expected to furnish cake and sandwiches for a midnight lunch, coffee for which is supplied by the owner of the farm.

"The music at these dances is usually that of a fiddle and mandolin, or a fiddle accompanied by the chording of an organ. Country people have a strong prejudice in favor of their own fiddlers who play by ear—the term 'violinist' being applied with some contempt to those that play by note. Some of the older 'fiddlers' of the community have real musical talent, and do play with a fire and smoothness of time much superior to the playing of many 'violinists.'

"The floors upon which we dance are rarely of

hardwood—and often of unmatched lumber. Waxing is accomplished by cutting up and scattering paraffin which is 'danced in.' One of the floors on which I had the privilege of dancing affords me a unique memory. I was at the warming of a little one-room log house, in which the floor joists were round green elm timbers. When we danced a lively 'Schottische,' in approximate synchronism with the period of vibration of the timbers, there was at least six inches of spring in the middle of the floor!"

But, too, there was always more work to go back to. Karl's farming life had begun with the cutting down of trees—piling logs on skidways, transferring the logs from skidways to a sleigh, and then driving the horse-drawn sleigh to market, often in the face of the sharp winds of sub-zero weather.

As the timber farm was transformed into a dairy farm, with hay fields and grain fields and pasture land, the size of the herd of dairy cattle was increased. Then milking and the care and breeding of cows became the major chore, for the economy of the whole area was geared to the processing of dairy products.

In the earlier years of dairy farming in Clark County, the big cans of milk, kept chilled in a large tank of running water piped from a well in the yard, were collected by dealers and shipped by train to be sold in Chicago. Then, as the area became more populated, small independently operated cheese factories became a feature of every neighborhood. The milk from each farm was then hauled by the farmers for a distance of two or three miles to be used for making cheese.

Karl learned something from every aspect of his life in Wisconsin. Most important for his future life, though, was the opportunity given him to observe the strange and variegated workings of nature. As if to confound those of his teachers who had feared that his experiences in Wisconsin would destroy his scholarly career, one of his projects on the farm gave him the material for his first published scientific paper, which eventually appeared in *The Nature Study Review* in March 1917. Appropriately, for a future herpetologist, it concerned a snake.

With the encouragement of his mother, Karl and the other children had become interested in the cold-blooded animals around the farm, the reptiles and amphibians. They acquainted themselves with the different kinds of turtles in nearby streams and lakes, with the green frogs along the creek banks, and with the leopard frogs that abounded in the cattail swamps. Karl learned to identify the springtime singing of the little swamp tree frog, whose annual choruses on the banks of the Wolf River could be heard all across the mile of intervening fields to the house.

Karl got to know the common kinds of snakes that turned up on the farm. He was fascinated by the defensive behavior of the blowsnake or puff adder, which was much feared by the farmers in the neighborhood. Karl did his best to dispel this fear of the puff adder and other non-poisonous reptiles. In fact, that was part of the reason for capturing the pine snake about which he was to write his paper.

The pine snake was caught in July. From its stockiness, Karl judged it to be a female with eggs.

It hadn't resisted capture as most pine snakes did, but once in its glass-fronted cage it tried continually to escape, instead of becoming sluggish and "tame," as was usual. It so mangled its nose, pushing against the glass, that Karl would have let it go if he had not hoped to see the egg laying. The first eggs appeared while two young women of the neighborhood, whose fear of snakes Karl was trying to conquer, were watching, fascinated even though they expressed disgust. The initial eggs were laid at intervals of ten minutes, but the interval constantly increased, so that it took four hours for all fifteen eggs to be laid. The young women, of course, were still watching at the very end. The sticky eggs, as long as pigeon eggs and about half as broad as they were long, unfortunately didn't develop. But the snake still proved interesting, for, after it had laid its eggs, it began to accept food, in the form of live field mice, the first of Karl's captured snakes to do so.

"The snake threw itself on the mouse," Karl later wrote in his article, "grasping it by the shoulder with the jaws, and coiled around it with the middle portion of the body. The body followed the head so quickly that separate motions of striking and constriction could not be distinguished. After a few minutes of constriction, so tight that the mouse's eyes bulged out of their sockets, the hold was released, and the mouse proved to be quite dead. The snake nosed its prey until it found the head, and immediately began the swallowing process. The remarkable mechanism of a snake's jaws whereby unbelievably large objects can be swallowed, is

32

easily observed. First one side and then the other of the separate lower jaws is moved forward, while the backward pointing teeth of the upper jaw, and of the inactive half of the lower, retain all that is gained. The snake literally draws itself over its food."

Karl continued to feed the snake; and it accepted twenty-one mice from August 16th to September 7th. A number of young field mice "were taken directly from the fingers, with no striking or constriction, and swallowed head or tail or back foremost as was convenient." Then, toward the end of August the snake began to get sluggish. Its eyes became opaque, and it accepted only young field mice, the larger ones being left undisturbed or killed but not eaten. On September 15th, the snake, with a little assistance from Karl, shed its old skin. Its eyes were bright again, and the new skin brilliant with its black and yellow pattern. And Karl released it from its cage.

Karl's years on the Wisconsin farm were almost at an end, although he would continue to return for brief periods. Contrary to the fears of his teachers, it had proved an experience which had stimulated him further toward a scientific career. In fact, it was what he had learned about the natural environment of the farm that would make it possible for him to return to school. He had lost nothing but time, and what he had gained in knowledge more than made up for that.

3
A Decision in the Swamps

"Good luck, Karl!"

Karl, dancing with a pretty girl from a new farm in the area, smiled and said, "Thank you."

The going-away party that was being given for him by his many friends from miles around was one of the best parties Karl could remember. The bows of the fiddlers zipped and zinged across the strings of their instruments, while the mandolins plinked faster and faster, and the dancers whirled below the high rafters of the barn. As always, the square dance was the favorite, but it was regularly alternated with waltzes and two-steps, even though some of the youngsters refused to attempt them. At one point in the evening, a true Scandinavian "hopwaltz" was played, giving some of the older people a chance to show that they could dance as rousingly as any of their children. The music surged, the dancers spun, and the noise created by so much gaiety seemed almost enough to lift the roof right off the barn.

Karl had danced just about every dance, it seemed, and he was glad when it came time for the midnight supper of sandwiches and cake furnished by the girls and women of the surrounding farms. But he hardly had a chance to wolf down even a sandwich or two, for he was kept busy replying to all his friends crowded around to wish him a good trip and a successful year.

"Be glad to get back to college, will you, Karl?"

"Oh, yes, sir," Karl said.

"And you won't miss farming, I'll bet."

"Well, I'll be teaching about farming, you see."

"Good for you, boy. At Cornell, is that right?"

"That's right," said Karl, and smiled again.

Then the music began once more, and Karl went back to dancing just as hard as before, even though he had a long train trip ahead of him in the next twenty-four hours, all the way to Ithaca, New York, where, on the bluffs above Lake Cayuga, Cornell University was located.

That Karl was going to Cornell was due almost entirely to Dr. James G. Needham, who had been Karl's biology teacher at Lake Forest College. During that same summer of 1907 in which the Schmidt family left Lake Forest for northern Wisconsin, Professor Needham had accepted a position at Cornell, one of America's greatest universities. There he was to teach the first college course in limnology, and later would create a new Department of Limnology and Entomology in the College of Agriculture. He was a very busy man, but he didn't forget his exceptional student from Lake Forest. Professor Needham corresponded with both Karl and his father during the following years, making repeated efforts to persuade his former student to return to school.

But for six years, the predicament of the Schmidt family made further schooling for Karl impossible. Until the timberland was cleared, the fields cultivated, and the dairy herd built up, Karl's presence was essential to the running of the farm. Hired men were employed, it was true, but they were often transients, and soon moved restlessly on to other jobs; or else they saved their money and bought their own farms. And, even if Karl could have been spared from the work of the farm, the family couldn't have afforded to send him back to college.

By 1913, though, the farm was fully operational, and it seemed possible that it could be smoothly run even in Karl's absence. Professor Needham came up with the solution to the other half of the problem, for he was at last in a position to provide Karl with a job that would pay most of his college expenses. He offered him a teaching assistantship, one of seven, in the new elementary course he was giving, a course which was to be required of all freshmen in the College of Agriculture.

With the exception of Karl, all the young men assisting with this course would be graduate students. But Professor Needham had no doubts concerning Karl's qualifications, for the course was entitled "The Natural History of the Farm." Karl's lack of an undergraduate degree and of certain prerequisite studies were more than compensated

37

for by his six years of firsthand experience with the subject matter. Thus, in the end, Karl's time in the wilderness bore double fruit: out of that wilderness a farm had been created, and the knowledge gained in that process was now to be the key to his return to academic life.

Writing an essay for his English course a few weeks later, Karl commented on the educational aspect of his years in Wisconsin: "During those six years, the life that appealed to me most was that of a *student* of the nature with which I was in intimate contact, the life of a field naturalist; and . . . I have entered here with the hope of finding companionship among those with interests like mine, and a chance to study."

He had come to the right place. For, in 1913, probably no other American university could have provided such an imposing faculty or as many students with interests like Karl's. Cornell was in the midst of a period of great expansion in all branches of the natural sciences. Students of botany, zoology, entomology, geology, paleontology, and agriculture were coming to Cornell from all parts of the United States, and from many foreign countries as well. With nearly five thousand students, Cornell was second only to Columbia University in enrollment and in number of academic courses.

Because of his maturity (Karl was 23), his family background, and his teaching assistantship, Karl was always identified with the student elite, the graduate students, rather than with the more numerous undergraduates with whom he was academically affiliated. Professor Needham had offered Karl a place to live without cost, a ground-floor room at 6 Needham Place, his own family residence; and, from the time of his arrival, the Needhams treated Karl as though he were a member of the family. He was often included at dinner when distinguished guests were present. And he himself was a frequent guest at the homes of several of his professors, who became his friends as well as his teachers.

Due to his wide range of interests, Karl was attracted to several different fields of study during his first year at Cornell. He registered for English I, comparative religion, entomology, botany, geology, and invertebrate paleontology. Although he was very interested in chemistry too, he found that the fees for courses in that department were much too high for his limited budget.

Karl was particularly excited by his studies in geology and paleontology, and he decided to make historical geology his college major. On the farm he'd always been intrigued by the unusual rocks and boulders that were everywhere so numerous; and one of the things that made his geology class such a pleasure was to be constantly finding answers to hundreds of questions that had bothered him for years.

Through his course in invertebrate paleontology Karl came into daily contact with one of Cornell's most notable teachers, Professor G. D. Harris. In his class he became familiar with the extensive fossil collection in the museum in McGraw

Hall, and quickly formed a warm and lasting friendship with Professor Harris' most gifted student, Axel Olsson.

Classroom instruction was only a part of Professor Harris' course. For many years it had been the Geology Department's policy to provide advanced students with summer excursions in the field, where they could study various geological formations, and where they themselves could collect the rocks and fossils which they would study later in the laboratory.

Since his special interest was in the geology and paleontology of the coastal plain of the United States, Professor Harris had built a sturdy thirty-foot cabin cruiser for field work with his students. The cruiser, called the *Ecphora,* had sleeping accomodations for five, besides himself. To Karl's delight, Professor Harris invited him to join the 1914 summer field trip.

With Karl as engineer, Axel Olsson as cook and electrician, and a crew of three other students, the group set out in the *Ecphora* on a calm morning in June. That year their destination was the tertiary deposits along the shores of Chesapeake Bay, which they reached through an obsolete but still usable network of state and privately owned barge canals. After a five-hour run that first day, they reached the town of Cayuga, at the lower end of the lake. The ponderous bridge of the New York Central Railway was raised for them to pass, and when it had dropped behind them they were in the canal system of the State of New York.

The branch canal joined the historic Erie Waterway at Montezuma, with a rise of about eleven feet in two small locks. They found it advantageous, in going up, to have two men ashore, handling the ropes from bow and stern that were necessary to hold the *Ecphora* steady, while two others of the crew wielded pike poles from aboard the boat, and a fifth man handled the wheel. The waters entered the lock with a rush, and would have crushed or wrenched the boat disastrously if it had turned sideways.

Passing down the Erie Waterway, through various further locks and on into the Hudson River, gliding eventually past Manhattan, its towers rising dimly through a foggy dawn, they finally entered the New Jersey canal system at Perth Amboy. New Brunswick, Princeton, Camden, and Philadelphia were left astern. At Wilmington, Delaware, they picked up a dinghy for use in shallow southern waters. The middle of that afternoon found them in the first of the three locks of the Delaware and Chesapeake Canal, whose thirteen miles connected the lower Delaware with the upper end of the Chesapeake Bay.

"The speed limit of four and a half miles per hour is rigidly enforced on this canal," Karl wrote after the expedition. "But time spent on it was not regretted, for the southern influence made plant and animal life extremely interesting to our party of Northerners. The banks at many places open out into wide lagoons thickly overgrown with lily pads, where fish rose and frogs croaked at their king, the apparently impassive blue heron, standing in the shallows. Turtles sunned themselves on the sandy canal bank, dropping into the water at our approach. Minks, living a life of plenty behind the wooden lining of the canal, showed themselves to us even by daylight. Cardinals and Carolina wrens dominated the shrubbery of the banks, and impressed on us the fact that we were indeed entering the naturalist's land of promise, the South."

Next morning rounding Turkey Point and catching a glimpse up the Susquehanna River, they entered Chesapeake Bay. Not until August did they return from their explorations of the area, bringing back with them an extensive collection of rock sections and fossils. For his enthusiastic participation in this field course, as for each of the other nine courses in geology and paleontology that he took at Cornell, Karl received a grade of 95, or "A."

In September of 1914, Karl began his junior year of college (his second year at Cornell) by registering for a course in entomology, one in zoology, another in Spanish, and for four courses in geology and paleontology. He continued to assist Professor Needham with his course on "The Natural History of the Farm," and to live at the Needham residence. But an unexpected development was to take Karl away from the campus for the entire second semester of that year, and to change the course of his life.

In February of 1915, at the beginning of the spring term, Professor Harris called Karl into his office and told him of an opening for a well-site geologist with the Pardee Oil Company, in Louisiana. Professor Harris recommended the job, for it would provide Karl with valuable field experience,

and at the same time would enable him to earn some extra money toward his college expenses. Karl gladly accepted the offer, and left immediately for the south.

Karl's duties, upon his arrival at Chastine Well number I in western Louisiana, were to wash the cuttings from the rotary drill and to collect any fossils, label them, and then to box them up and ship them back to the museum in McGraw Hall. But there weren't any fossils, not in all the thousands of feet of clay and rock which the Pardee Company's team drilled through—nothing except for a single piece of oyster shell. Still, the trip would not be wasted. For even if there were no fossil remains of creatures long dead, there could hardly have been more live ones to absorb Karl's attention.

That far south, it was already spring. The swamps and woodlands surrounding the tiny oil-drilling camp at Chastine were full of snakes—more of them every day, it seemed. Salamanders and ground skinks darted in the undergrowth, tree frogs squatted blinking on branches, and lamp eels slithered through the grassy waters. There were few places in the world where Karl could have found such an incredible abundance of reptiles and amphibians, and it was the best time of the year to study them. So, as often as possible, Karl left the oil camp and set off deeper into the swampland, collecting as many specimens as he could, and constantly watching and listening as all around him the snakes and lizards of western Louisiana wakened to spring. After dark, during the hours he might have spent labeling fossils, he went out into the night

44

instead, in order to observe and to collect the emerging frogs and toads, as one species after another appeared in succession through the early spring, all of them chorusing loudly across the murky swamps.

Before this trip to Louisiana, Karl hadn't received very much instruction in the preservation and care of biological material. His field training had been mostly in relation to his studies in geology. But after it began to appear that there were going to be few fossils to collect, Karl wrote to his friend and teacher Professor A. H. Wright for advice on the collecting of biological specimens, particularly reptiles and amphibians. To Karl's delight, Professor Wright sent not only a series of letters giving detailed instructions on the techniques of collecting, and for making valid field observations, but he also shipped several boxes of equipment to Karl, including a generous supply of the most important preservative solution used by field naturalists—formaldehyde.

And so Karl set about gathering together a kind of collection other than the one he had originally intended to make. What was more, he began to realize that this new collection interested him even more than the fossils might have. "I don't know," he wrote in a letter to Professor Wright, "whether or not I will ever get to the point where each separate capture of a snake is not an Adventure." And he didn't capture just green garter snakes and southern black racers, but a number of poisonous snakes as well—copperheads, water moccasins, and a coral snake. Most exciting of all, he managed to catch new kinds of water snakes and blue racers unlike any that had ever been described by any naturalist in the world. Many of these snakes were collected by shooting them, but some were taken alive.

Once, moving cautiously forward through the woods, Karl paused to turn over a likely looking log with his foot. And sure enough, coiled there in a disused mole burrow was a spotted snake about a foot and a half long. Karl immediately attempted to imprison it with a forked stick he was carrying with him. Curiously, the snake appeared to go into convulsions. Then, abruptly, it collapsed, its mouth wide open and its tongue hanging out. At the same time, its neck and body spread to almost double their original width, as though bloated in death. But Karl knew that he had trapped a spreading adder, and that the snake was only "playing dead," for self-protection. Karl waited, ready to bear down again with his stick. At last, furtively, the snake began to move. Karl didn't even make use of his stick this time, but simply moved one of his feet, and instantly the snake returned to playing dead. It was a fascinating game, Karl thought.

And then there were the lizards: "Their delicate coloration, their graceful forms, their lightning movements, the comical expressions of their faces, and their ludicrous courting antics, furnish the most delightful memories of the south," Karl wrote. Always there was something new to absorb him: a different species from those he had already captured, or behavior he hadn't previously observed in a species he did know. He'd seen many examples of

the common green lizard, for instance, but it wasn't until April 11 that he observed the expansion of the red throat fan of the species. On that date he caught sight of a large specimen at the base of a small tree, climbing upward by stages of about a foot at a time. Between each period of forward movement, the lizard paused, raising and lowering the front end of his body, and at the same time extending his bright red throat fan in jerks that were synchronized with the bobbing of his body. The local children, Karl discovered, spoke of the lizard as "showing his money" when he engaged in this performance, and Karl observed it with amusement many times after that day.

There was so much to discover, about all these creatures inhabiting the swamplands, that it seemed a shame to Karl that his adventure ever had to end. Still, he was at Chastine for four months in that spring of 1915, from February to June, and by the time he was ready to return to Cornell he'd captured 111 snakes, 132 lizards, twenty-one turtles, and eighty-seven frogs and toads, and that was just part of his collection. In his notebooks he had the information to write a first-rate term paper. But the most important result of his months in the swamps and woodlands around Chastine was a decision that would change his life.

Karl had gone to Louisiana as a student geologist; but, by the time he had to leave, he had come to the conclusion that what he really wanted to be was not a geologist at all, even a geologist who might find much more interesting things than a single piece of oyster shell. The swamps of western Louisiana, slithering and squirming to life that spring, had taught him that what he really wanted to be was a herpetologist—to make the study of reptiles and amphibians his lifework.

4
A Coming of Age in Herpetology

Karl glanced out his porthole. Through the pearly dawn light the prominent hill that formed the northwest boundary of the open harbor of Monte-cristi rose out of the sea. It was Karl's first glimpse of the island of Santo Domingo, which is now called the Dominican Republic.

Karl and his friend Axel Olsson rushed up to the deck of the S.S. *Algonquin*, the Clyde Line steamer that had brought them from New York. The steamer was letting down its anchor, with a great clanging. Leaning on the rail, Karl and Axel watched the small boats setting out toward the steamer from the single pier. The harbor was much too shallow and the pier too small for the steamer to approach any closer to land.

"I wonder how serious this revolution that's supposed to be going on really is," said Axel Olsson. "It would be awfully disappointing if we couldn't get to the interior after coming all this way."

"Well, we'll see the American consul first thing," Karl replied, "and just hope for the best."

It was the fifth of May, 1916, almost a year from the time when Karl had decided, in the swamps of Chastine, that he really wanted to be a herpetologist and not a geologist. Yet here he was on another expedition from Cornell that was primarily geological. Not that Karl was unhappy about it. He was still interested in geology. What was more, in the course of the expedition he would be able to do some herpetological collecting on the side. That was what he had done the previous summer, too, when, immediately after his return to Cornell from Louisiana, he had joined Professor Harris on the *Ecphora* for a second field trip. They had travelled down the same route to Chesapeake Bay, but had continued on further, into the Carolinas. And on that trip, when he wasn't collecting fossils or rock sections, Karl had found time to make a good enough collection of Carolina reptiles and amphibians that during the fall he was able to write his first herpetological research report.

This research report was written for a course called "Advanced Systematic and Field Zoology," given by his friend Professor Wright, who had supplied Karl with instructions and materials in Louisiana. The report was called "A Contribution to the Herpetology of North Carolina;" and in the process of writing it, Karl learned a lot more about what it meant to be a herpetologist. His notes made in the Carolinas on some fifty specimens representing twenty-nine different species were sufficient for a "faunal-list" type of paper, in which the species were listed and related to their distinctive habitats.

In trying to determine the proper scientific names of his specimens, Karl learned to apply the methods of a systematic zoologist. He found that it was necessary to compare particular traits or features (called *characters*) in order to discover whether or not they differed from those that were designated as "species determining" by leading authorities in herpetology. If, for instance, the pattern and coloration of the spots on a snake differed in character from those of any known snake previously listed by a herpetologist, then it might be that he had discovered a new species or sub-species of snake.

In making such comparisons, of course, Karl found it necessary to do a lot of digging into scholarly books and periodicals—reading all the "literature" about his specimens. And the distinctions between one species and another were so fine that the use of a microscope or a dissecting knife was generally required. This kind of research confirmed Karl's determination to be a herpetologist, for he found it even more exciting than collecting in the field.

That fall of 1915, after his return from Chastine and the *Ecphora* expedition to the Carolinas, Karl had asked about the possibility of transferring as a teaching assistant to the zoology department. But an undergraduate can't very well switch majors in his senior year—Karl's degree would have to be in geology. Still, he was able to take Professor Wright's zoology course; and, after he had written his paper on North Carolina for it, he began an even more ambitious project.

This new project, entitled "Notes on the Herpetology of Northern Natchitoches Parish, Louisiana," was a detailed discussion of the reptiles and amphibians at Chastine. Consisting of 123 typed pages and six illustrations, it listed the many kinds of snakes, frogs, salamanders, turtles, and lizards to be found in one square mile of Louisiana swampland, and described their complex relationship with their environment. Professor Wright was so favorably impressed with the scientific importance of this report that he thought it worthy of publication in the scientific papers of the Smithsonian Institution, and sent it to his colleague Dr. Leonard Stejneger at the United States National Museum.

Karl had no sooner completed this report than Professor Harris offered him another job as a field geologist. Karl seemed to be embarked on a double career! This time, if he were interested, he would be sent together with his friend Axel Olsson to explore the fossil beds in the northern part of Santo Domingo. If he were to go, however, it would mean that he would lose a term of college study, and so would be unable to graduate with his class in June. On the other hand, the trip would take him to a herpetologically fascinating tropical island in the Caribbean Sea. Moreover, while on the expedition he would be allowed to collect reptiles and amphibians as well as fossils. Karl accepted the proposal at once.

And so here he was, in the city of Montecristi, a mile inland from the harbor, a city where, as Karl wrote, "The unshaded streets, the dust, the reflections from the tin roofs, the quivering atmosphere, testify to the heat of a tropical desert, and seem to intensify it by making it visible." Karl and Axel sought out the American consul, who assured them that revolutions of one sort or another went on all the time, that there was nothing to worry about, and that they could safely proceed on their expedition to the interior. In fact, however, this particular revolution *was* something to worry about; but the two young men from Cornell did not find this out until some time later.

Karl had learned to make careful preparations before going on collecting trips, so that he would be ready for anything that might turn up. There were a number of different tools that could be useful in capturing herpetological specimens. Salamanders and lizards (and sometimes frogs and snakes) were often found beneath old logs, or under rocks. To assist in rock turning and logrolling, Karl would take along a light crowbar, or sometimes a short-handled hoe. (In order to leave a suitable habitat for some other specimen, though, he made it a point to replace any logs or stones or other objects that were disturbed during his explorations.)

For capturing snakes, Karl discovered that his most useful tool was a four- to six-foot pole with an iron hook or angle iron firmly fastened to one end. The snake could be scooped up quickly by the iron hook, then seized behind the head and thrown deftly into a snake bag—a small muslin or light canvas bag with a drawstring, one bag being used for each specimen. The specimens collected during a trip were taken back to camp or the laboratory in a larger, sturdier collecting bag, carried over the shoulder. Salamanders and frogs were placed in moist collecting bags, or sometimes in wide-mouthed jars. All these methods were commonly used by the herpetologists of the time.

When it came to catching poisonous snakes, Karl employed the usual long pole with a noose of wire or leather dangling at one end. The noose could be opened and closed by a stiff wire or rod running the length of the pole and held firmly to it by wire staples. After "noosing" his catch, he would pull on the stiff wire to tighten the loop around the snake's neck. A poisonous snake was always killed immediately, by injecting formalin solution or alcohol directly into the heart. Then Karl would drop the snake into a jar or metal container filled with more of the formalin solution. This preserving solution is made by mixing commercial thirty-seven percent formaldehyde with water in the ratio of one part formaldehyde to ten parts of water. Returning to his camp or laboratory after a few hours or a day in the field, Karl always injected more of the preservative solution into the body cavity and muscular parts of his specimens, using a large hypodermic needle. If the snake were very large, he would follow the usual procedure of opening its body cavity by making long cuts in the underside. The openings would allow the perservative fluid to enter every part of the specimen and prevent its decomposition.

Salamanders, lizards, frogs, and turtles were preserved in much the same way as snakes, and with the same kind of formalin solution. During the first few days that his specimens were in the solution, Karl would check to make sure they were "setting" or "hardening" properly. If any part remained soft, the specimen would require further opening, or transference to a fresh preservative solution. Specimens were often "pinned," while hardening, in paraffin-lined trays, immersed in preservative. Finally, for permanent storage of preserved specimens, Karl again followed the practice of other herpetologists and transferred his specimens from the formalin solution to eighty percent alcohol.

Killing salamanders, small lizards and frogs, and turtles was the same as killing snakes—the preservative was injected directly into the region of the heart with a hypodermic needle.

In addition to carrying collecting bags and smaller snake bags and glass jars, Karl usually wore a cartridge belt or hunter's vest filled with bullet-sized glass vials that had cork or rubber stoppers. Small specimens, whether lizards or tree frogs, or even scorpions and spiders, were always placed in these little vials, along with a proper label for each one. And, finally, Karl often carried a smooth-bore pistol that fired rifle cartridges loaded with dust-shot. The dust-shot was so fine that it caused very little damage to the specimens—yet as his career progressed Karl would become a good enough shot to hit every specimen at twenty feet!

Since the Dominican expedition was primarily a geological one, requiring an entirely different kind of equipment, Karl and Axel were well weighted down by the time they set off into the interior on horseback with their native guide, Lalo. Riding southeast and stopping frequently to take geological specimens, they progressed toward the central valley of the island. Karl collected herpetological specimens whenever he had a chance, his most fruitful collecting being done along the Gurabo River. Here, he found large pure green tree lizards, and tiny geckos which lived beneath the loose outer bark of trees. Six species of snakes were collected by Karl and Axel on the river banks, or were brought to them by the small native boys whose keen-eyed help Karl had enlisted. There was one species of tree snake that Karl found particularly handsome, brilliant green with a sharply defined white and golden line on each side. It sometimes reached an extraordinary length, and one brought to them at Los Quemados was nearly six feet long. But their longest snake of all was a boa constrictor.

"I don't believe it," said Karl, and nearly burst out laughing.

He and Axel were cooking a simple evening meal of a fish they had caught in the Gurabo. Karl looked up at a sound in the brush, and saw approaching them out of the palm trees a tiny naked urchin who was dragging by the head a boa constrictor nearly seven feet in length. The snake was dead, of course, and the child had found it that way, but still it was an extraordinary sight. In Spanish Karl thanked the child and as he was so small and the snake so large, gave him double the usual reward of five cents in Dominican currency. The urchin took the money gravely, and scampered away into the palms again.

As they travelled onward, Karl and Axel heard more and more rumors that the uprising which the

American consul had told them not to worry about might after all be serious. Often their guide Lalo had to make complicated explanations about the expedition to suspicious natives. They were supposed to return to Montecristi before setting off again in a new direction; and as they neared the city they passed numerous solitary armed men who would question Lalo ominously. When at last they reached Montecristi, they discovered they had returned none too soon. The revolutionaries had started shooting, and all Americans were ordered to take refuge aboard the United States gunboat *Panther*, where they remained for four days. Karl and Axel still hoped to reach Santiago for further explorations, but it wasn't possible. As Karl himself later wrote, "Conditions in the interior were such that we were most urgently advised to abandon the attempt to reach Santiago, since Desiderio (the rebel leader) was entrenched there, and geologizing in the lonely thickets would certainly result in our being shot and never heard of again. The sight of seven dead men on the pier at Macoris convinced us that this was no idle fancy." And so the expedition was over.

Even so, they returned to New York with dozens of boxes filled with Dominican fossils—hundreds of species of fossil molluscs, crustaceans, echinoderms, and corals. And, too, they had Karl's considerable collection of reptiles and amphibians, preserved in many cans of alcohol.

While he was in New York, Karl decided to visit the curator in charge of one of the country's largest scientific collections of reptiles and amphibians—

Mary C. Dickerson, at the American Museum of Natural History. For many months Karl had wanted to meet Miss Dickerson and to see the great collection under her care. But he had a special reason to see her now. He knew that his days at Cornell were ended, and he was concerned about his Dominican collection. Perhaps Miss Dickerson would be willing to write a scientific report on this material.

At any rate, as soon as he and Axel could get back to Ithaca with their collections, Karl knew he would be packing his belongings and returning to the farm in Wisconsin. He had no funds or assistantships with which to continue his education any farther—at least not now. And his help was urgently needed at home.

At the time of Karl's visit to her laboratory, 50-year-old Mary Cynthia Dickerson had been in charge of the museum's herpetological collection for nearly eight years. She had shown a remarkable ability for expanding the collection, and a special knack for discovering fresh scientific talent. During Karl's brief visit, she was much impressed by the professional maturity of her young visitor from Cornell. She agreed to look over his Dominican specimens and to write a report on the collection if the specimens and notes were worthy of the time such a study would require.

A day or two later, Karl and Axel reached Ithaca with the collections from their expedition. Karl immediately began preparations to leave for Wisconsin. With Professor Wright's permission, he repacked the reptiles and amphibians from Santo Domingo and shipped them home with his books and other belongings. He needed time to label his specimens more completely before sending them on to Miss Dickerson, and he knew he could do the job in his spare time at home. Besides, the specimens would be a reminder, as he worked on them, of the scientific life to which he knew he must return, and which would somehow have to be reconciled with his responsibilities to his family and the farm.

One evening soon after returning to Wisconsin, he came into the house hot and tired from cutting alfalfa with a scythe all afternoon, and found a post office notice informing him that the shipment of the Dominican specimens had become lost in transit and might never be found.

Karl slumped down in a chair. His back ached, and his eyes felt red and prickly from so much sun. There were thirty acres of alfalfa out there waiting to be cut, and he had the help only of his brother Frank and one hired man. His spirits had been sustained by the hope that his Caribbean material would attract the attention of Miss Dickerson and merit a scientific report. Now that hope seemed gone, and he felt suddenly exhausted.

"All that effort, gone to waste," he muttered.

"Don't despair, Karl," his mother admonished. "It may all turn up yet."

And, in fact, it did, before the end of July, and in perfect condition. By the middle of August, Miss Dickerson had received Karl's shipment of the carefully labeled specimens, together with his detailed notes on the color, habits, and distribution of the many specimens.

As soon as she had examined Karl's specimens

and notes, Mary Dickerson was convinced that the young farmer-student was a true "find" for the science of herpetology. She immediately asked herself how she could bring the exceptional talents of this young herpetologist into the service of her museum. In her opinion, Karl should himself write the report on his Dominican specimens. But to do this properly would require the facilities of a suitable museum.

It was several weeks before Mary Dickerson found an answer to her problem. But it finally occurred to her that a year earlier two of her colleagues, Herbert M. Lang and James P. Chapin, had returned from the Belgian Congo with an unusually large collection of reptiles and amphibians. This collection was still unpacked in the museum's storeroom for uncatalogued material.

After consulting with Dr. Frederick A. Lucas, director of the museum, and winning his encouragement and support, Miss Dickerson decided to try to bring Karl Schmidt to New York as her assistant, to unpack, catalogue, and perhaps to prepare a report on the herpetological collection of the American Museum's Congo Expedition.

But museum collections are of secondary importance in times of war, and by the fall of 1916 the United States was beginning to feel the effects of the war in Europe. Funds became more limited. Mary Dickerson could offer Karl a salary of only $75 a month, and she could promise him only three months employment. Would he come to New York under these discouraging terms?

"My dear Miss Dickerson," Karl wrote on October 16th, "I received today Miss Field's letter with your offer for three months work at the museum. It approaches too nearly to 'heart's desire' to think of refusing it . . . Needless to say, I am looking forward to the time of my life."

Karl couldn't possibly have overestimated his opportunity. After spending six years in the Belgian Congo, ornithologist James Chapin and herpetologist Herbert Lang had returned with the most important collection of reptiles and amphibians that had ever been assembled by an African expedition. Not only was the collection large—Karl would find it included more than four thousand specimens—but it was remarkable in other respects, too. All the material was excellently preserved; furthermore, it was accompanied by extensive field notes and exact locality labels.

But perhaps Karl's greatest advantage was his day-to-day consultation with the men who had made this remarkable collection. They were more than cordial—they were an inspiration. In his new work, Karl was also constantly encouraged by Mary Dickerson. And it was at her insistence that he registered for two additional courses at Cornell, which would win him his degree in June, 1917.

With the resources of such an excellent collection, the availability of the scientists who had formed it, and the exceptional library facilities of the American Museum, Karl was challenged to produce a report that would be of considerable scientific merit. But if the outlook seemed bright, at the same time he was faced with serious difficulties, both professional and personal.

In the first place, it was necessary for him to complete a great deal of bibliographical work in order to proceed with the study. This was because no comprehensive report on African herpetology had been done for twenty-five years, and references to the literature were scattered in many publications. Secondly, his work was greatly handicapped by a lack of African material for comparison. He was permitted to visit museums in Philadelphia and at Harvard University, and to borrow from their collections as well as from the small African collections of two or three other American museums. But in the end he found that his best comparison material was contained in the Congo collection itself.

Karl's personal difficulties as he proceeded with the study were more serious. His appointment was due to expire in February, but, happily, it was renewed for another three months. But he and Miss Dickerson knew that it would take much longer than that to bring the study to completion. As they feared, Karl's work was halted in April—Miss Dickerson had no more funds available. Hoping to remain in New York until his museum appointment could again be renewed, Karl succeeded in finding a job with the New York Sanitary Commission, as an entomologist. But in July this position was abolished, and he returned to Wisconsin again—just in time to begin harvesting the hay.

About the time that Karl's work at the museum was broken off, the United States entered the war against Germany. It would be many months before this country could get an army into the field, but even so Karl expected, from week to week, to hear from his draft board that he had been selected for induction.

Then, in October, Karl received a telegram from Mary Dickerson: AFRICA IS YOURS. SALARY, $150 PER MONTH. I HOPE YOU CAN COME.

"What are you looking so happy about?" asked his brother Frank, coming into the room.

"Just look," replied Karl, and handed him the telegram.

A few days later, Karl was again in the herpetological laboratory in New York, working feverishly on the Congo collection. "Am scairt to death now that I am here that my [draft call] to be ready on twenty-four hours notice will arrive by the next mail," he wrote to his mother on November 1. "Every day it stays away, however, justifies the venture. I have no difficulty in taking up the work where I left off, and am crowding it for all I am worth."

On November 25 he wrote, "I feel that the gods have been real decent in postponing the fatal slip that is to call me to Rockford [Camp Grant]. I have the last species of lizard described, but I still need a good deal of time for distribution maps and revision. Here's hoping I can get it polished off! If I have more time, I will take a little vacation from Africa and revise my Louisiana paper for publication here."

Triumphantly on March 3, 1918, Karl wrote again to his mother: "I handed in my paper Friday, and am enormously relieved. It will secure my place in the museum as absolutely nothing else could, and it has been commented upon favorably by nearly everyone who has seen it. I wish I could be here to superintend publication, but I suppose that is too much to expect . . . I can now arrange to leave here on a few hours notice, and I shall look forward to it with some degree of tranquility."

A few weeks later Karl was inducted into the United States Army, at Camp Grant. Before saying good-bye to her industrious assistant, Mary Dickerson assured him she would send on the printer's page proofs of his monograph, for him to correct and return. Numbering nearly 250 pages, with twenty-five plates, twenty-two maps, and twenty-seven text figures, Part I of his *Contributions to the Herpetology of the Belgian Congo* would be a lasting reminder of his first real job as a herpetologist.

5
A Developing Career

Once again Karl stood at the rail of a ship as it slid into a harbor at dawn. This time, though, it was not Axel Olsson who stood beside him, but rather his bride of only a few weeks, Margaret Wightman Schmidt. Lying before them in the dim light was the walled city of San Juan, Puerto Rico. It was August 3, 1919.

Karl had met Margaret Wightman during his eight months in the Army. Camp Grant, where he served as a sergeant-major, wasn't far from his boyhood home of Lake Forest, and he had many relatives in the area—including some second cousins near Wheatland, at whose home he was introduced to Margaret. The war in Europe was nearly over even at the time Karl was inducted into the Army, and he was never sent overseas. On Thanksgiving Day, 1918, along with thousands of his fellow-soldiers, he received his discharge. And by early February of 1919, after visiting Margaret at college and dealing with some family matters, Karl was once again at his desk in the herpetology department of the American Museum of Natural History, in New York. He had been given a salary raise, and his title had been changed from that of research assistant to "Assistant Curator of Herpetology."

He set to work at once on Part II of his *Herpetology of The Belgian Congo*. In this final portion of his study, he would deal exclusively with the snakes of that region. As in Part I, dealing with the turtles, crocodiles, lizards, and chameleons, Karl would do much more with his material than merely list the different species that had been collected, or simply note their habits, coloration, or other descriptive features. In great detail, he worked out the geographic distribution of the snakes, drawing distribution maps for each species on the basis of the extensive specimens and detailed field notes that had been so thoroughly collected by ornithologist James Chapin and herpetologist Herbert Lang. And on the basis of his study he was able to arrive at some general conclusions about the why's and wherefore's of reptilian distribution on the continent of Africa. He could demonstrate, for example, the way in which the reptiles of the grasslands were distributed all around the great rain forest that almost divides Africa into two sub-continents. In making such generalizations from his study, Karl would be achieving the goal of every true scientist—to relate his specific data to the broader principles of science, thus adding to the world's fund of scientific understanding.

As time permitted, Karl also began work on a scientific report of the excellent collection of reptiles and amphibians that he had made while on the geological expedition with Axel Olsson in the Dominican Republic during the summer of 1916. The collection was actually the property of Cornell University, which had sponsored the expedition, but it was still in the laboratory of Mary C. Dickerson at the American Museum. Miss Dickerson, who at Karl's request had agreed to write the report, had postponed starting on the project in the hope that Karl himself would someday be able to do it. And at last that was possible.

While Karl was concerned with his Congo study and his Dominican material, Miss Dickerson was making plans for some still more important scientific work for him to do. For several years, the New York Academy of Sciences had been sponsoring an extensive scientific survey of tropical Puerto Rico and the Virgin Islands in the West Indies. Leading geologists, botanists, entomologists, and other natural scientists of this country had been commissioned by the Academy to conduct expeditions to the region and to prepare detailed reports of their studies.

Miss Dickerson knew that the Academy was looking for an expert on reptiles and amphibians to conduct a herpetological survey as part of its Puerto Rican program. Sitting at her desk one day, it suddenly occurred to her that Karl was just the man for the job. And in July of 1919 she sent a letter to Dr. Nathaniel Britton, the famous botanist who was President of the Academy, recommending that Karl be given this important scientific assignment on the basis of his Dominican studies and his skill as a scientist and field naturalist.

To the delight of both Miss Dickerson and Karl, he was selected by the Academy for the job. What's more, it would be possible for his bride of only a few weeks (Karl and Margaret had been married following her graduation from Oberlin College) to accompany him on the expedition.

And so, leaving the rail of the S.S. *Coamo* that early morning of August 3, 1919, the young couple disembarked, and took the streetcar to their hotel in the suburb of Turce, overlooking the tropical sea. Margaret Schmidt shared her husband's excitement about the expedition, which was the first Karl had made in which the study and collecting of reptiles and amphibians was his primary objective. Karl was particularly interested in the fact that there was such a variety of habitats to be explored in Puerto Rico and its small neighboring islands. "Puerto Rico," he wrote, "includes a wide range of habitat conditions, from the extremely wet mountain rain forest of the Luguillo, where the mountain palms and hardwoods are hung with lianas and draped with moss that never dries out, to the opposite extreme of aridity on the southwest corner of the island (near Guanica and Ensinada) where a cactus flora predominates."

The rain forest provided ideal conditions for tree frogs, and Karl found that they were almost incred-

70

ibly abundant in the moist belt above 1200 feet. "The amphibian chorus on El Yunque," he wrote, "is the most extraordinary I have heard. As one stands at the Forester's Cabin, at about 1300 feet altitude, a roar of sound comes from the wooded ravine adjoining, and from the slopes above, making a veritable Babel of frog notes."

Karl set about trying to distinguish between all these sounds, and to discover which sounds came from particular frogs. One insistent note turned out to belong not to a frog but to a grasshopper, while another note, sounding just like that of a grasshopper, proved after all to come from a frog. "A sad little series of whistles descending on the scale and becoming successively fainter," Karl noted, "proves to belong to a very distinct species of small *Eleutherodactylus* which sits on the ground or the lower leaves of plants, and is certainly a most difficult species to discern even when it is singing a foot away from the collector's ear."

Their most unusual specimen was captured in a habitat of the opposite extreme, in the tableland of Mona Island. The sun beat down out of a torrid sky on the exploring party. The natives Karl had hired to assist him wore several pieces of pigskin strapped to the soles of their feet, to protect them against the knife-like edges and spear-like points of the weathered limestone. Even so, Karl was astounded by their agility as they threaded their way through the cactus plants which grew in the handfuls of soil that existed in the small hollows of the tableland. His own shoes, he realized, would be demolished by the end of the day's tramp.

71

Suddenly there was a howling from the dogs up ahead. The natives rushed forward. At last they had a prize! A giant ground iguana, more than three feet long (and eventually found to weigh over nine pounds), had been caught and wounded by the dogs. It seemed in that moment almost as though the clock had been turned back a hundred million years, for here was a creature that might have come right out of the Age of Dinosaurs.

That single specimen was the only one seen by the party of seven men in an eleven-hour tramp, but the native hunters reported that the rock iguanas took refuge in cracks and holes in the rock, and were somewhat more abundant than that day's experience indicated. No such rock iguanas existed on Puerto Rico itself, but Karl found that the bones of a fossil species were common in cave deposits.

The sharply contrasting types of habitat which Karl explored on Puerto Rico and its neighboring islands stimulated further his growing interest in the question of geographical distribution of reptiles and amphibians. This was not just a matter of listing the particular kinds of specimens to be found in certain conditions of climate and terrain, but led to the broader questions of why a given kind of snake, for instance, should be found in one sort of habitat and not in another. In many cases, there was also the question of *how* a certain specimen had gotten to its present habitat. On an island, the presence of a particular species which was much more common on the mainland might suggest the possiblity that, eons before, the island had been connected to the mainland by a ridge of land now sunk beneath the sea. Thus, questions of herpetology might be answered by the application of geology, or some other branch of the sciences.

The Schmidts were in Puerto Rico and the adjacent islands of Mona, Vieques, and Culebra for only two months, from August 3 to October 8, but even so Karl was able to obtain a total of 1,253 specimens. His first purely herpetological expedition had proved a great success. Yet it was to be three years before Karl would again be part of a field expedition. In the meantime, he and Margaret, after their return from Puerto Rico, spent several months on the farm in Wisconsin, helping his parents. Returning to New York and to science, Karl spent another year at the Museum of Natural History. But then, in 1922, Karl accepted a job at the new white marble headquarters of the famous Field Museum in Chicago, whose original collection had so fascinated him as a small boy. And it was here, in the city he had loved as a child, that he was to spend the rest of his professional life.

In the beginning, Karl's title was Assistant Curator of Reptiles, but his job was bigger than his title. He was in charge of a newly created department containing a reference collection of eight thousand reptiles and amphibians. Still, this herpetological collection was small when compared with those of several other great museums. Accordingly, one of Karl's principal jobs would be to enlarge the reference collections—to obtain more frogs, lizards, turtles, snakes, salamanders, and crocodiles, together with the pertinent scientific information about them. And since the scope of the Field Museum was

73

world wide, Karl was challenged to obtain specimens from all parts of the globe.

Within a year from the day of his appointment to the staff, the collection of eight thousand specimens had grown to nearly twelve thousand. A few hundred of these were collected by Karl from the Chicago area; several hundred more were received as gifts; and some were purchased. But most of the four thousand additions were acquired by the Field Museum's expeditions.

For increasing its collections, in numbers and in importance, the Field Museum has always depended primarily on its expeditions. In 1922, the year Karl joined the staff, the museum sent out twelve major expeditions. The next year twelve more were sponsored. Seven of these went to South America, the others to China, the Malay Peninsula, the Gulf Region of the United States, and to Central America.

The expedition to Central America, known as the Captain Marshall Field Expedition to British Honduras and Honduras, was led by Karl. It was his first for the Field Museum. Significantly, this expedition exemplified the two major interests of a museum of natural history—acquiring specimens for the exhibition halls, and acquiring specimens for the increase of scientific knowledge.

Accompanied by museum taxidermist Leon Walters, Karl sailed from New Orleans on January 18, 1923. The expedition spent five weeks in British Honduras. Here they obtained a rare "lost" species of crocodile that hadn't been collected for more than fifty years. Then, sailing on to Honduras, they

collected amphibians, reptiles, fish, birds, and mammals in the tropical lowlands as well as in the rain forests, at altitudes above 4,500 feet. They returned to Chicago on June 2 with 1,625 specimens, more than fifty large plastic molds of crocodiles (casts from these molds would be made with cellulose acetate, which were later built up from the inside, over many months, into lifelike models), together with other materials for an exhibition group of crocodiles in habitat, and notebooks crammed with scientific information.

This exhibition once again extended Karl's interest in the geographic distribution of reptiles and amphibians. As must always be the case in the observational sciences, Karl arrived at general conclusions through observation of the particular: "At night a note like isolated strokes on a tiny silver bell was heard on all sides of us. It was extremely difficult to trace, but proved to belong to a tree frog which was frequently found in the bases of the bromeliaceous air plants."

This pinpointing of that isolated note in the rain forest of Honduras led to a further discovery—the hyla (tree frog) was engaged in laying its eggs in the water contained at the bases of the leaves of the plant. Later, in the laboratory, the hyla proved to be a previously undescribed species.

These same air plants were also found to be the home of two kinds of salamanders, one of them red and the other covered with lichen-like markings, and both kinds were again proved to be new species.

Specific observations of this sort led Karl to write,

76

in more general terms, "It was borne upon us even in the field that we had discovered a mountain top whose animals composed a distinct fauna, isolated in the distinctive cloud-forest conditions from the same zone on other mountains by the broad river valleys to north and south. It is one of the simplest and most striking principles of species formation—and in other words of active evolution—that isolation of any kind, in insular patches of cloud-forest quite as much as on oceanic islands, is accompanied by the development of distinct forms of animals confined to such areas."

Three years later, Karl's second important expedition for the Field Museum, the Captain Marshall Field Expedition to Brazil, brought him still further scientific information on which to base his developing ideas about geographic distribution. On this expedition, he explored the vast marshes along the upper reaches of the Paraguay River in an area of Brazil known as the Pantanal. Here he was able to observe the huge floating mats of vegetation, known as *camelotte,* which were "composed principally of a coarse grass, with finger-thick stems, and two or three kinds of water hyacinth." These mats of vegetation were carried by the current, like rafts, thousands of miles down the Paraguay River to the South Atlantic Ocean, causing the dispersion of numerous species of animals and plants all along the length of the river.

It was while he was on this expedition that Karl Schmidt began work on what was to be one of his most important projects, a translation into English, and a revision, of Richard Hesse's *Ecological Foun-*

77

dations of Animal Geography. There was no really adequate work in English on animal distribution, and Karl hoped to fill the gap with this book. His explorations of the extremely varied habitats of Puerto Rico; his discovery of numerous isolated species on the forested mountaintop in Honduras; and his observation of the great raft-like *camelotte* in Brazil had all contributed to the understanding of geographic distribution that would make this book important.

6
The Great Voyage

Karl Schmidt paused for a moment on the windy pier in the harbor of Boston, Massachusetts, and smiled once again at the sight of the huge sailing vessel tied up alongside. Her name was lettered proudly along her bow: *Illyria*. The wind tugged at the collar of Karl's coat, and he moved on toward the gangway. It was mid-November 1928, and in a few hours Karl would be sailing aboard the *Illyria* on a year-long expedition to the South Pacific. Richard T. Crane, a member of the board of trustees of the Field Museum in Chicago, had made a gift of the *Illyria* to his son Cornelius, the sponsor and leader of the expedition. She was a beautiful ship, designed and built especially for this voyage— it could not have been accomplished otherwise.

Supported by an all-steel hull, the 147-foot-long.

thirty-foot-wide ship had a three hundred-horse-power engine to keep her under way when the winds were too gentle to fill her sails. As well as comfortable staterooms, there were well-equipped laboratories for studying and preserving specimens, and a special darkroom for the expedition's photographers. The *Illyria* was even equipped to convert ocean water unto fresh water, by condensation, as a supplement to the forty-one tons of water she carried aboard. Forty-one tons was the capacity of the reserve fuel tanks for the diesel motor, as well. And below decks were an enormous refrigerator and large storerooms stocked with enough food to last for six months.

Karl was to command the scientific explorations during the long voyage. He knew that it would probably be the most important field expedition of his life, and he'd begun his preparations months in advance. He had prepared lists of the zoological specimens needed to fill the gaps in the museum's reference collection, and had then studied maps of the South Pacific to determine where the needed examples might best be collected. From the museum library he made a careful selection of books that might be needed by him or his colleagues for checking scientific data—such scholarly works were not likely to be very available in the jungles of Pacific islands! Conferring constantly with Cornelius Crane and officials of the museum, Karl sent letters to foreign offices to prepare the way for the expedition's eventual arrival, and talked or corresponded with all the men with whom he would be working during the year of exploration.

Now, at last, on November 16, under Captain S. B. Boutilier, the *Illyria* was sailing. She had a crew of sixteen sailors, engineers, cooks, stewards, a mess boy, and a radio operator. Her small company of "explorers," besides Cornelius Crane and Karl Schmidt, included artist and ornithologist Walter A. Weber of the Field Museum; Frank C. Wonder, taxidermist, also of the Field Museum; Dr. Albert Herre, an ichthyologist from Stanford University; and Dr. W. L. Moss, physician, Sidney Shurcliff, photographer; Charles Peavy, and Murray Fairbank, all Harvard classmates of Cornelius Crane.

Before entering the Pacific, through the Panama Canal, the *Illyria* put in at Hamilton, the capital of Bermuda, and then at Port-su-Prince, seaport city of Haiti. At Hamilton, Karl and Frank Wonder collected the first specimens of the expedition—tree frogs, gathered from the shrubs around their hotel.

"It just goes to show that you can start a herpetological collection right in your own backyard, doesn't it?" said Karl. And he added, joking, "Maybe we shouldn't bother to go to the South Pacific, after all."

But their next find was further out of the way, in an abandoned quarry on the outskirts of Hamilton. Here they discovered several lizards and a female specimen of the remarkable Bermudian frog, which lays its eggs on land, under rocks. The eggs develop without passing through the tadpole stage, in water, as do the frogs of North America. When Karl and Frank examined the eggs they'd collected, they could see that the embryo frogs inside their transparent envelopes were nearly ready to hatch.

81

"I think Walter Weber should see these," Karl suggested.

Walter Weber did come to take a look, and immediately sat down to make a watercolor sketch of both the eggs and the mother frog. Cooperation between the members of such an expedition, making use of all the available skills and talents, means that a much more thorough record can be kept than is possible with a one- or two-man expedition—like the one Karl made with his friend Axel Olsson to the Dominican Republic when he was still at Cornell.

Leaving Hamilton, and after a brief stop at Port-au-Prince (where Karl and Frank collected a series of small birds and lizards), the *Illyria* set course for the Panama Canal, which was entered on December 11. From the day of leaving Boston, the ship's crew had had trouble with the generator and the refrigerator. Minor repairs had been made on this equipment in Bermuda and again in Haiti, but before reaching Panama the engineers decided that a major overhaul was necessary. So, after passing through the Canal, the *Illyria* docked at Balboa, on the Pacific side, for the repair work. To the dismay of most members of the expedition, the engineers found that the mechanical problems would keep them docked for three weeks.

"Never mind," said Karl. "I think we can make it a worth-while stopover, even so." He had remembered the existence of Barro Colorado Island!

As every American naturalist knows, Barro Colorado Island, in the middle of the Panama Canal Zone's Gatun Lake, is one of the finest examples of

82

an untouched tropical jungle in the western hemisphere. The island is especially interesting to zoologists because of the variety of animal life—tropical birds, monkeys, iguanas, jaguars, anteaters, and insects—that had migrated to it when the nearby lowlands were flooded to make Gatum Lake and the Panama Canal. The entire island is preserved as the Canal Zone Biological Area, and is equipped with a laboratory for visiting scientists.

Actually, there was nothing sensational about the collections that were made on Barro Colorado Island by the visitors from the stranded *Illyria*. But good museums are not based just on unusual specimens. What Karl wanted, in this case, was to complete sets or series of island and mainland specimens he'd previously collected in the American tropics. Taken together, these sets would provide reference material Karl would need for comparison with other island-mainland forms he hoped to collect in the southwest Pacific. Strong as his interest remained in herpetology, in reptiles and amphibians, Karl had developed, as well, a keen interest in the distribution of all animals over the world—the science of zoogeography. Even during his years as a student at Cornell, and as a freshman curator in New York, he had been fascinated by the questions of animal geography. And, like Charles Darwin and Alfred Russel Wallace and many other students of animal evolution, Karl Schmidt had realized that he must go to the tropics to observe the continuing processes of evolution under the most favorable conditions. Thus the specimens he took on Barro Colorado Island, when related to mainland animals, were a kind of preparation for island-mainland relationships he expected to come upon later in the South Pacific, where special conditions of the environment had caused unique forms to evolve.

But even though some good work had been accomplished on Barro Colorado Island, all members of the expedition were very glad when the *Illyria* was at last ready to sail westward on December 29. With two blasts from her whistle, she swung from her Balboa dock out into the vast Pacific. The true size of that ocean would not impress itself upon them until later, though, for their first destination was less than four days' sail from Balboa. On New Year's Day, 1929, surrounded by a school of porpoises and dozens of frigate birds, the *Illyria* entered beautiful Chatham Bay, on the shores of Cocos Island. Cocos, in actuality a group of mountaintops pushing skyward from the sea, was one of the last strongholds of maurauding pirates in the 1700's, and visitors may still read the names of old sea dogs carved on the rocky bluffs. But Karl and his companions were interested, not in pirate treasure, but treasure for science. They set out to discover whether above and behind the boulder-studded coast of Cocos lay hidden natural history data which could contribute to the knowledge of evolution and zoogeography.

For Karl, Frank Wonder, and Walter Weber, the treasure hunt meant piling into the *Illyria's* motorboat, and cruising along the rugged shore collecting marine shells, hermit crabs, fiddler crabs, and spiders; working up a rocky stream, climbing over slippery boulders; or scaling steep cliffs to the high

84

green ridge to college birds and lizards. For ichthyologist Herre, the museum treasure hunt meant dropping charges of dynamite into Chatham Bay, then gathering in the fishes stunned by the underwater explosion—the first collecting he'd done since leaving Boston. His finest specimens were coal-black trigger fish, with blue lines at the bases of their fins, and surgeon fish, with knife-blade devices on their tails that could be unfolded for slashing other fish to ribbons. Finally, for Dr. Moss, the search meant wild-pig hunting, and the capture of a black and white sow with a curious "mane" on her shoulders.

While the collectors went about their work, expedition leader Cornelius Crane and photographer Sidney Shurcliff set out to explore a steep-sided valley with a high waterfall at the far end. Unfortunately, they encountered only trouble. First, Cornelius was badly bruised and winded by a twenty-foot fall from a rocky cliff; then both were nearly drowned in the overpowering surf before they could be rescued by their companions.

In spite of this near-tragedy, Karl concluded that scientifically, at least, the Cocos stop had been worthwhile. Along with Dr. Herre's fish specimens and the wild pig obtained by Dr. Moss, a fine series of the island's little tree-climbing iguanas was taken, as were several birds found only on Cocos.

As the *Illyria* sailed away from Cocos, porpoises again played around her. Karl was talking to Captain Boutilier on the bridge. Suddenly, a large porpoise jumped high out of the water, landing again on the surface with a report like a pistol shot. Karl smiled, and thought back to the night before they had reached Cocos, when across the dark water glowing streaks of pale phosphoresence had marked the wake of the ever-roaming porpoises.

Such unexpected delights were part of the pleasure of every expedition. Karl had learned that many years ago, during his first trip with Professor Harris' *Ecphora*, down through the canal systems of New York and New Jersey to Chesapeake Bay. Equally exciting, for Karl, were the delights of looking ahead, of anticipating new regions yet to be explored. Now, as the *Illyria* once again sailed westward, Karl's expectation was particularly sharp, for in two days they would reach the Galapagos Islands. From the time when the first plans for the expedition had been made, Karl had known that the Galapagos would prove one of the most stimulating and rewarding stops along their entire route.

Since 1835, when they were visited and studied for a month by Charles Darwin, the father of evolutionary theory, the Galapagos Islands have been fascinating to naturalists. The important point about these islands is that they first appeared centuries ago as active volcanoes. Once bleak and dead, they have gradually been coming to life with their own distinctive kinds of plants and animals. A sanctuary for wild life, this naturalist's paradise is inhabited by gigantic land tortoises (which are unfortunately becoming extinct, for not every unique form of life proves lasting—in fact the most unusual are often the most quickly doomed). But there are also sea iguanas, strange rodents, and many unusual

birds, such as flightless comorants. The shore lagoons teem with colorful, exotic fishes, with club-spined sea urchins, writhing and twisting sea worms, starfish with snake-like arms, scarlet crabs, brilliant shell-less molluscs, sponges, and sea fans.

Writing to his family in Illinois, Karl said, "It would take a volume to write all of our experiences in the Galapagos Islands." Continuing, he wrote, "So far as general natural history is concerned, the most interesting thing on the coasts was the illustration of how land plants and animals get a foothold even on such barren and glassy rock. First comes the animal and plant life of the ocean. Shells of snails and clams and crabs are pounded up by the surf into sand, and worked into the crevices and hollows of the lava, sometimes quite far inland by storms and high tides. Then comes the mangrove, with its floating seeds and ability to live in salt water. It gets a footing wherever there is sand. Its leaves blow into crevices and a tiny bit of humus is formed. This is fertilized further by lizard and bird dung, lizards and birds getting their food from the sea. Next come the few true land plants that can gain a foothold—a grass, a sedge, a cactus, and one woody bush. Flies appear, breeding in excrement and in the dead bodies of birds and lizards, and spiders are then able to make a living, stretching their webs between the upstanding points of lava, or from a cactus to a bit of lava. Wood-boring beetles are able to live on the dead mangrove. All the forms that depend on the sea seem in place, but it is strange to find the rats, which perhaps have turned crab-eaters, as have the small lizards."

Later in the same letter he described the famous flightless cormorant, a bird in which the never-ending process of evolution was strikingly apparent. "The flightless cormorant, which we came to see as much as any bird, was everywhere abundant. All other cormorants are good fliers, but here, with no enemies and no reason to fly because of the constant abundance of food, the wings of the local cormorant have become reduced to the stage of complete uselessness."

The expedition spent ten days in the Galapagos— not as long a time as they could have liked, but long enough, to absorb many lessons in evolution and zoogeography from the unusual islands. Their next stop would be the Marquesas, three thousand miles further across the Pacific, a journey that would take them three full weeks. And so on January 17, at 5 a.m., the *Illyria* left the shelter of the Galapagos, sailing westward once again.

The long voyage to the Marquesas allowed the explorers a generous stretch of time for studying and preserving specimens, for reading, for card playing—and for writing. Always one to make the most of such spare time, Karl had set aside this "recess" for a specific job—completing the revision and translation into English of Richard Hesse's book *Ecological Foundations of Animal Geography,* the work that he had begun while he was on the Brazilian expedition in 1926. If the work progressed as he hoped, he would have it nearly completed by the time he returned to Chicago, in the fall. Actually, the book was being written in collaboration with his friend and colleague, Professor Clyde Allee

89

of the University of Chicago. One of America's most noted animal ecologists, Professor Allee had given Karl much encouragement and help from the first days of Karl's employment at the Field Museum. Together, with the permission of Professor Hesse, the two would produce a study that would fill an important gap in the scholarly material available to American zoologists in English.

Chapter 12 of this book, the section Karl was now writing, was about the animal populations of the ocean, and especially the communities of animals that live along the coastal areas of warm seas where the conditions for life's development are most favorable. How appropriate, Karl thought, that this part of the book should be his concern at this particular time. For he wanted, after all, to base his writing on first-hand experience, on what he had seen with his own eyes, as well as on what had been seen and reported by others. Underlying the paragraphs he was writing about the rich animal population in thickets of seaweed, with their worms, starfish, carnivorous snails, sea anemones, and sea urchins, were his fresh memories of what he'd seen and collected in the Galapagos. This was true, also of the section of "mangrove associations," assemblages of oysters, fiddler and hermit crabs, mudskipper fish, and certain aquatic birds and reptiles, diverse animals woven into a single complex biological relationship. And Karl knew that before he'd completed the section on coral reefs and atolls and coral islands he would have had first-hand experience with them, too, in the Tuamotu Islands en route to Tahiti.

The Crane Expedition sailed on through the South Pacific to Tahiti, the Fiji Islands, the New Hebrides, the Solomon Islands, and then to Borneo, where it concluded its itinerary on June 27. After leaving the *Illyria,* Karl, Walter Weber, and Frank Wonder spent ten days collecting in northern Borneo, then went to the Philippines, where they collected near Zamboanga. They returned to the United States by way of Manila, reaching Chicago on September 3. All these places brought the explorers new adventures—too many to describe. For Karl, though, one of the most interesting stops was in New Guinea, where the *Illyria* made a two-week voyage up the flooded Sepik River, traveling almost four hundred water miles inland.

On May 11, 1929, on the Sepik, Karl wrote: "We spent a couple of hours at a river village, Bien, nine miles below Marienberg, photographing and purchasing some of their extraordinary carvings. I was lucky to run onto a captive baby crocodile, which seems to be my new species (of last year), *crocodilus novae-guineae.* It is certainly a unique experience to describe a new crocodile from anthropological specimens and then go out and collect the animal itself!"

What's more, Karl was fascinated to discover that the canoes of many of the inland tribes had bows carved like crocodile heads. In fact, even some of their houses were built in the shape of crocodiles. The great clubhouses, occupied by the unmarried men, were particularly impressive. The main part of each building formed the body, while the overhanging "prow" at one end outlined the head of the animal, mouth wide open, and the other end tapered to resemble a crocodile's long tail. "I hunted geckos one night in one of these—a weird experience," Karl wrote his family.

By the end of the year of the Crane Expedition's voyage, the total specimens collected for the Field Museum included twelve thousand fishes, two thousand reptiles and amphibians, one thousand two hundred birds, one thousand mammals, and some two thousand insects, crustaceans, worms, molluscs, termites, and enchinoderms.

Karl went on another major expedition for the Field Museum in 1933-34, the Mandel Expedition to Guatemala. And in 1939 he led the museum's expedition to Peru and the Magellanic Islands, off the coast of Chile. But the Crane Expedition, the great voyage to the South Pacific, remained the most extraordinary of them all.

7
Karl P. Schmidt, Naturalist-Author

Expeditions to far places in the constant search for both usual and unusual specimens were an important and certainly an exciting part of Karl Schmidt's career with the Field Museum. But there was another side to his work, too. However far he voyaged, he returned always to his laboratory and desk to write about where he had been and what he had seen there. In technical terms he would write for his fellow-scientists. In more popular terms he would write for the general public. The knowledge for which Karl Schmidt often journeyed such distances was not brought back just to sit in either his head or his laboratory. Karl took pains to see that it travelled outwards again, the further the better, through his magazine articles, museum bulletins. exhibits, books, and scientific reports.

Compared with other naturalists of his generation, Karl was an exceptionally productive writer and museum teacher. What's more, he was exceptionally versatile. He felt that museum naturalists were the *humanists* among scientists—middlemen between the unfamiliar, sometimes frightening technicalities of science and the general public. In particular, he felt that it was the duty of museum naturalists to encourage and promote a widespread interest in the natural world.

There are many reasons for the scientist to write for the general public as well as for other scientists. One very basic and important reason can be illustrated by the first popular article Karl ever wrote, the one about his pet pine snake in Wisconsin—to "keel a supersteeshun" (kill a superstition), which in this case meant trying to correct a widespread illusion that all snakes were harmful. Another good reason, for a naturalist in particular, is to protect an animal species or a nature sanctuary in danger of destruction. For instance, the first article that Karl wrote after beginning his job at the Field Museum was on the American alligator, arguing against the ruthless slaughter of this reptile in the swamps of the south.

Then, too, there were broader questions, which Karl tried to answer. At the Field Museum he was often asked, "How can a person become a naturalist?" So he wrote a series of articles on the subject, suggesting first of all that students get acquainted with a few great naturalists by reading their biographies.* And he went on to discuss some of the most

* These articles were first published in 1943 in *The Chicago Naturalist*, and later issued as a bulletin of the Chicago Academy of Sciences.

appealing of them, listing books that could be found in any public library. He also recommended books about the travels of naturalists, both the classic works by the great naturalists of the past, and some of the more important modern books. He included the writings of artist-naturalists, like John James Audubon and Louis Agassiz Fuertes, and photographer-naturalists like C. B. Schilling, A. R. Dugmore, and F. W. Champion, as well as the works of scientist-authors such as William Beebe and C. M. Yonge.

From time to time Karl wrote magazine articles about his own travels—to the guano islands of Peru, the cloud forests of Honduras, the high Andes, the rivers of Central America, or the mountains of northern Mexico. Because the topics they deal with are not often discussed by other writers, these articles will always appeal to readers who go to the small trouble of looking them up in back issues of *The Chicago Naturalist, The Texas Geographic Magazine,* and *The Scientific Monthly.*

Yet, however interesting his other works might be, Karl himself considered his most important writings for the general public to be his articles, museum bulletins, and books on frogs, toads, salamanders, turtles, and snakes, those curious creatures whose full fascination he had discovered as a young man in the swamps of Chastine. Although these creatures were often regarded as offensive and even frightening, Karl knew that they were really endlessly interesting; and in many popular writings he made them seem so to the general reader.

Karl wrote a great deal for the general public, for

people who were not scientists, but it is only fair to say that he wrote even more for the scientists themselves—for herpetologists, ecologists, and animal geographers. To begin with, he wrote often about the classification of reptiles and amphibians—a subject which is technically called *taxonomy*. A herpetological taxonomist is a museum scientist who is qualified to classify a newly discovered kind of reptile or amphibian into the right species and to give that species its new scientific name.

An expert taxonomist, Karl wrote seventy-five or more articles concerning new species of reptiles and amphibians. Published in various scientific journals, neither the titles nor the contents of these articles is easy for the non-scientist to understand. But by shifting from technical words to everyday language, it's possible to see why to other herpetologists Karl's taxonomic studies are of such great interest. In everyday language some of these would read: "Ground Lizards from the West Indies," "A New Kind of Earless Lizard from North America," "A New Skink from the Islands of the Western Pacific." "New Sheep-frogs from the High Andes," "A New Toad From Korea."

From the viewpoint of other naturalists, Karl's most important scientific writings probably were what might be called his "regional studies"—his various reports on the reptiles and amphibians of individual countries, or islands, or still more limited areas of the world. Based on both the specimens he himself had collected and those collected by others, these regional studies will long stand as a kind of monument to Karl's memory. Printed in many important scientific journals and special museum bulletins, they are still used by museum and university herpetologists all over the world. They are wonderfully diverse in their treatment of kinds of species and in their geographic range. A glance at some of their titles illustrates Karl's world-wide interests: "Amphibians and Reptiles of the Big Bend Region of Texas," 'Some New and Rare Amphibians and Reptiles from Cuba," "The Amphibians and Reptiles of Lower California," "The Lizards of the Marquesas Islands," "New Reptiles and a New Salamander from China." "Amphibians and Reptiles of Yemen (southwest Arabia)," "New Amphibians and Reptiles from Iran," "Herpetology of the Belgian Congo."

From the titles of these and other scientific reports, it would seem that Karl's interest in herpetology was always general, spread over the entire field from tadpoles to iguanas. But he was recognized by other research scientists not only as a generalist but also as a specialist, an expert on the coral snakes of the tropical Americas, and on the alligators and crocodiles and caimans of that part of the world as well. In fact, his scientific reports on crocodilians and on coral snakes are still among the most important studies of these animals that have yet been written.

Beyond these strictly herpetological interests, of course, Karl turned his attention more and more, over the years, to the science of zoogeography. Actually, a knowledge of the facts and theories about geographic distribution is part of the equipment of every museum scientist who studies plants or ani-

97

mals. This is particularly true of those who serve as curators in large museums. Each of them is occupied with special studies of certain species or other groups (such as genera and families) of plants or animals, but all are also concerned to know why these forms are found at one place on the earth rather than at another (under natural conditions).

Animal geographers, then, and plant geographers as well, are "theoretical" or 'explanatory" scientists who deal with the whole scheme of life on earth. Students of animal geography are interested in such matters as how climate affects animal populations— making it impossible, for instance, for moist-air breathers like snails and amphibians to live in the same places as dry-air breathers such as rattlesnakes and antelopes. They know that warm-blooded animals in cool regions grow larger than the same species in warmer climates. They know that in tropical climates cold-blooded animals are as favorably conditioned as warm-blooded species, attaining their greatest size, their most brilliant colors, and their greatest number of species. And from such facts zoogeographers try to develop general theories about animal distribution.

As Karl's own interest in this field developed, it led him to the study of birds and mammals as well as reptiles and amphibians. In the Galapagos Islands, for instance, not only the giant land tortoises but also the flightless cormorant attracted his attention. It's not surprising, therefore, that in time he was promoted from chief curator of reptiles at the Field Museum to the position of chief curator of zoology. In this new position, to which he was appointed in 1941, he was able to advance further as a zoogeographer; and he published several noteworthy papers including a history of the science. And, during his years at the Field Museum, in addition to being the principal editor of all zoological papers published by the museum itself, he served at various times as herpetological editor of many of America's most important magazines of natural history, including *Copeia* and *Biological Abstracts.*

From boyhood, Karl's enquiring mind had constantly led him on into new fields and greater knowledge, from history to historical geology, from geology to herpetology (thanks to the swamps of Chastine), and from herpetology to zoogeography. He was never satisfied with just the job at hand. He would do that job well, but alwa;ָ he looked around him to see if there weren't a further job he could take on too. Another young man finding that the work he had been sent to do didn't really exist, as Karl found at the oil-drilling camp in Chastine, might just have been discouraged and done nothing. However, that's not the kind of man who becomes curator of zoology at a great museum.

But a man's success, especially in the museum field, is not based only on intellectual curiosity and industry. The same qualities of personality which brought Karl a happy family life gave him also the friendship of many other naturalists. At the Field Museum itself he had particularly close and friendly relations with the artists, taxidermists, sculptors, and model makers who produced the museum's many exhibits. He always took an active part in the planning of exhibits on reptiles and amphibians, and other subjects as well, believing that good museum teaching required informative displays executed with the highest technical and artistic skill.

The young boy who lay on the grass in Chicago's Jackson Park in the first year of the twentieth century, wondering how he could ever see as much of the world as he wanted to, never lost that curiosity and enthusiasm. Karl Patterson Schmidt grew into a man who did in fact see a great deal of the world, on expeditions to many far places. But perhaps the most appropriate of his many successes as a naturalist was that he should have been responsible for so greatly enlarging the collections of the very museum which, in Jackson Park fifty years before, had been such a stimulus to the imagination of a young boy.

On September 24, 1957, more than two years after his retirement from the Field Museum, Karl Schmidt was identifying a snake for a zoo. The snake was a poisonous African boomslang. It was a young specimen and quite small, so that when it bit him, Karl merely sucked the fang-punctures on his left thumb and took no further steps to protect his health. If he had gone immediately to a doctor, an antidote to the bite of the boomslang might have been administered. As it was, Karl Patterson Schmidt died the next day.

Karl had been handling snakes for more than forty years without a serious mishap. Certainly he would have wished any young person with an interest in herpetology to understand that it was in large part his own fault that the bite of the boomslang proved fatal. Karl Schmidt's professional life was a long and extremely productive one, an inspiration to any young naturalist. He had put a great deal of thought and time into instructing the general public about herpetology. And he would have been the first to point out that the circumstances of his death held their lesson, too.

If it was a sad ending to Karl Schmidt's career, it could not in any way be called a tragic one. He had lived an unusually full and exciting life, and the pleasure that he took in it will continue to have its effect for many years, both through his own writings and through the teaching and writing of other, younger naturalists whose careers he assisted and inspired. Karl Patterson Schmidt saw and accomplished much, but his happiest achievement was to pass on to another generation both his great knowledge and his lasting curiosity about the natural world.

Nature Projects You Can Do

As a young naturalist interested in herpetology, you will want to observe frogs, toads, turtles, salamanders, and snakes in their natural surroundings. Of course, these animals aren't as commonly seen as insects or birds. Generally, they're found only in special places, and in order to observe them you'll have to tramp through swamps, hike through woody glens, climb along rocky ledges, or wander along the banks of streams and rivers. If you live in a rural area, especially in the southern part of the country, your opportunities for seeing reptiles and amphibians obviously will be much better than if you live in a town or city. But even though you may not live in the south or even in the country, with a little patience and persistence you can find at least some of the more common forms without much trouble.

When you go on nature hikes you'll discover that you can detect the eyes of a frog or the snout of a turtle above the surface of some quiet pond. You'll learn how to get close to a turtle sunning on a log, or a water snake swimming near shore. You can even learn to recognize frogs and toads without actually seeing them—by their wonderfully varied voices. Most libraries, schools, and museums have record albums from which you can learn to identify the calls of frogs and toads. Good books (some excellent ones are listed at the end of this section) can also help you prepare yourself so that a field trip will be truly rewarding. Visits to your nearest museum or zoo will give you an opportunity to get acquainted with various reptiles and amphibians so that when they are seen in the field or studied in books they will be old friends and easily identified.

On your actual field trips a good notebook is very important, as is the proper collecting equipment necessary for bringing back your live specimens. You are liable to have an opportunity for taking photographs, so that a camera is a good piece of special equipment to take with you. Finally, you will want a field guide to help you in making proper identification of reptiles and amphibians.

For your home museum, you will want to make a collection of preserved specimens for study, or casts for exhibit display. You should be very careful, however, about preserved specimens, as the preservative solutions used by museums are very poisonous—deadly when swallowed, and very painful to the eyes if you should rub your eyes after spilling the solution on your fingers. Secondly, the numbers of many salamanders, frogs, lizards, snakes, and turtles are now becoming limited. Some kinds are actually becoming rare. Accordingly, these animals shouldn't be killed unnecessarily, even by scientists. You will win the thanks of all professional naturalists if you study and enjoy these herpetological creatures, without trying to make large collections of preserved specimens.

There is however an interesting and valuable way to study amphibians such as salamanders, small frogs, and tree toads, and at the same time gradually to make a preserved collection. Arrange an aquarium with soil, damp mosses, and small woodland plants, including ferns. Keep your salamanders or other small specimens in this vivarium. As most small amphibians have rather short lives, even under good conditions and with proper feeding, some of your stock will die, quite naturally, and this will be your chance to start a preserved collection without having to kill anything yourself.

The purpose of this Nature Projects section is to help the young herpetologist make the most of his experiences in the field and to gain further knowledge and experience by visiting museums and zoos, developing his collection, and learning how to keep and care for live specimens. These are occupations which will provide many hours of adventure and enjoyment.

1. How to Find and Collect Reptiles and Amphibians in the Field

The beginning collector is advised to read over the paragraphs that follow and then to read further in books selected from the bibliography. In no case is it recommended that you go on a snake collecting expedition on your own if you have not been carefully instructed by an expert.

Equipment you will need: You should have several wide-mouthed jars which may be carried in a collecting bag. The jar lids should be perforated to admit air, and in them you should place some loose soil, leaf litter, or even moist paper towels. The jars will be used to contain any live frogs, toads, salamanders, or lizards that you may find. You should take along several small flour sacks, with stout drawstrings, to hold any harmless snakes you may succeed in catching. If you keep these small sacks moist, they can be used for holding live frogs, toads, and salamanders. Old pillowcases also make good snake bags. A broomstick or a modified golf club equipped with an iron hook or angle iron at one end is useful for catching snakes. A pole with a leather or wire noose can also be used, but it is difficult to catch a snake by this method without injuring it. (Snake sticks such as these are used to pin down the neck of the snake until it can be picked up behind the neck between thumb and forefinger.) A dip net is used for aquatic snakes and other reptiles. A light crowbar is useful for prying up stones or turning over logs, but a three- or four-prong potato rake is even better, for it can be used for pinning snakes as well. A hoe is also useful, as is a dip net for aquatic specimens. Last, but not least, a good pair of field glasses will allow you to watch at close range the drama of the daily lives of many reptiles and amphibians without the risk of frightening them away.

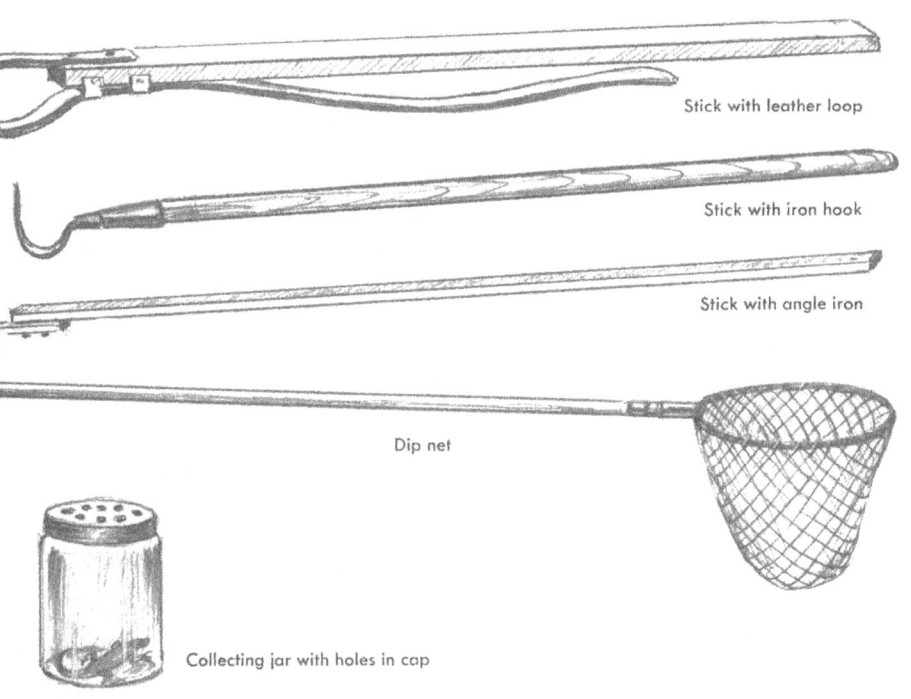

Stick with leather loop

Stick with iron hook

Stick with angle iron

Dip net

Collecting jar with holes in cap

Where to find reptiles and amphibians: It has already been mentioned that you must go to the woods and swamps and along stream banks. It's important that you go at the right time of the year, and at the right time of day, as well. Springtime is best of all. Rock turning and log rolling are favored techniques for finding these animals, although these must be done cautiously in areas where poisonous snakes are common. They are very dangerous in the southwest of the United States, although also very productive. Turn over pieces of bark, paper, old cans, in fact practically anything lying on the ground, always replacing such items so that you won't seriously disturb the natural conditions that enable these animals to live.

Night collecting of frogs and toads is particular fun. With a flashlight, or better yet a head-lamp, you'll be able to approach frogs and toads in the dark. They remain still when illuminated, and often can be captured by hand. But you must be as quiet as possible, for they are easily frightened by noise. You can often locate frogs and toads at night by their voices. Sometimes you'll find you can imitate their calls, and in this way get them to call back and tell you where they are.

When you go on field trips for reptiles and amphibians you do need to be careful of poisonous snakes. There is no point, however, in killing poisonous snakes that are found far from human dwellings. They must be recognized as important aspects of our wild-life heritage and treated accordingly. Your chances of being bitten by a poisonous snake are not very great. Just the same, the proper precautions should be taken.

In a few localities, poisonous snakes outnumber harmless snakes, but generally speaking this is rare. In fact only about eight per cent of the world's snakes are poisonous to man, and most of these live in the tropics. Within the United States, there are four major kinds of poisonous snakes: rattlesnakes, copperheads, cottonmouths, and coral snakes. However, there are more than twenty different kinds of rattlesnakes, the majority of which live in the American southwest and in northwest Mexico.

Every amateur naturalist and herpetologist should know something about treating the bites of poisonous snakes. The best thing to do, of course, is to keep the patient calm and quiet, and to get him to a doctor as quickly as possible. Only if it is impossible to get to a doctor within an hour should any attempt be made to treat the patient in the field. However, if that situation should arise, there are inexpensive first-aid kits for the treatment of snakebite which can be bought, and should perhaps be carried as part of your equipment if you live in an area where poisonous snakes are common. Such kits contain antivenin, a piece of

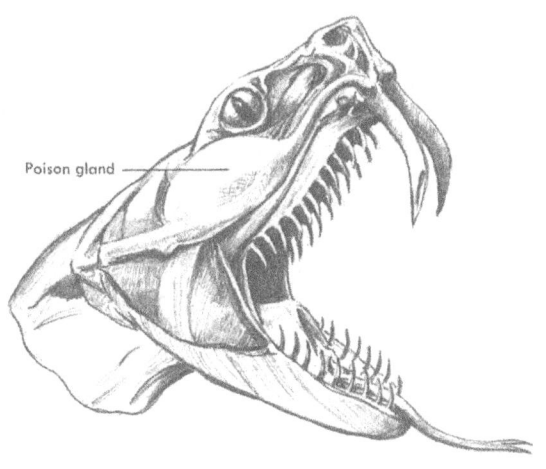

Poison gland

rubber hose to be used as a tourniquet, and usually a suction cup for drawing off the poison. But the use of antivenin without a doctor's supervision can be dangerous. Also, the old practice of using a surgical tool (sterilized over a flame) to make an incision over each fang mark is now regarded as unwise. Such incisions have been known to cut tendons or veins, and that kind of wound, or the loss of blood it might bring, could easily be more dangerous than the snakebite itself. Again, if at all possible, simply keep the patient from moving around too much, and get him to a doctor as fast as you can.

This information is given as a precaution. It should be repeated that your chances of being bitten are not very great. Long trousers and boots are of some protection, but it is a statistical fact that most snakebites are on the hands or arms—so that wearing gloves might be a good idea. But the best protection of all is simple care. In areas where poisonous snakes are common, you should be very careful when crawling under fences, reaching into cavities, and climbing bluffs. Common sense will do you a lot more good than a snakebite kit.

COPPERHEAD

TIMBER RATTLESNAKE

Red

Yellow

Black

CORAL SNAKE

COTTONMOUTH

2. Visiting Zoos and Museums of Natural History

In addition to observing reptiles and amphibians in nature, you should visit your nearest zoo, and your nearest museum of natural history. In each of these places you'll probably discover informative and interesting herpetological exhibits. If you happen to find some unusual specimen, make an entry in your field notebook (which you should always carry on expeditions) telling just where you found it, and take it to the curator of reptiles of a zoo or museum. This may be your ticket of admission to the herpetological research laboratory, and to a half-hour's conference with an expert naturalist. Always take along your field notebook when you visit zoos and museums; if you have a camera, take that too.

Some of the modern natural history museums and zoos and a good number of the children's museums and natural science centers have special classes for those interested in various aspects of natural history; find out about the one in your locality and become a member. Some museums and centers have junior curators or junior staff members who do advanced work in such subjects as herpetology, and if you join their classes you may have a great opportunity to get help and guidance in your field. Under these programs you will be able to go on field trips led by experts, usually curators at the museum or zoo. You may also be able to get professional advice on the care of your live exhibits, and assistance in the preparation of your own museum displays and research projects.

3. Caring for Captive Specimens

You can learn a great deal about reptiles and amphibians by keeping a few specimens in captivity. Many kinds make good pets. You should not keep any poisonous snakes as captive specimens, though, for they are too great a risk. In

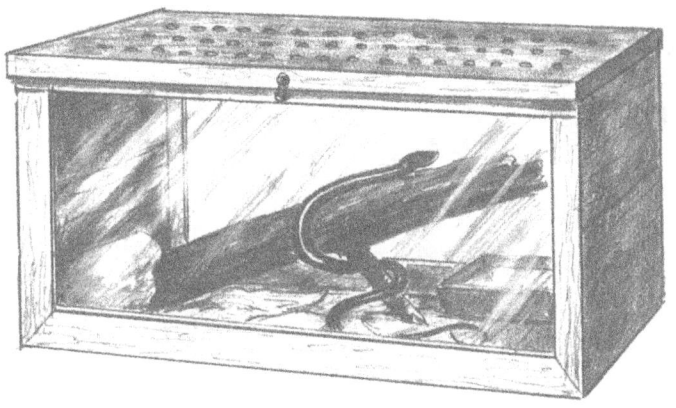

fact, most victims of snakebite are not field collectors, but handlers of captive poisonous snakes being kept in cages.

In general, snakes are harder to keep in captivity than are other reptiles and amphibians. They should be placed in dry cages which have been floored with newspaper. Newspaper helps prevent mites and chemical irritations, although for occasional display purposes you may want to use pebbles and sand as a floor covering. There should be some sticks for climbing purposes; and a hiding place should be supplied. Also, a dish or pan of water should be placed in every snake cage. A simple wooden box, with a glass pane on the front and a sturdy screen-wire or wire-mesh lid that can be firmly hooked or latched, is ideal. Snakes must be fed live food. The smaller kinds often eat insects, but most snakes must be fed mice or frogs—some will even eat eggs. In connection with the feeding of snakes, the temperature of the cage is important. Most snakes will not feed if the surrounding temperature is below 80° to 90°. You can use heating pads and light bulbs to help maintain that temperature.

Turtles are probably the easiest herpetological specimens to keep as pets. Baby turtles are the most popular of all.

Thousands of them are sold by pet shops every year. It must be added, though, that thousands die because of improper diet and heating. Their shells become soft, their eyes swell, and they die. Cod-liver oil and a beef diet, along with a cage temperature of 85°F, will sometimes correct these symptoms. For turtles and salamanders, and frogs as well, you should make an aqua-terrarium—an arrangement that provides both water and dry land. To make an aqua-terrarium you should buy a standard aquarium tank. Place soil or pebbles, or both, at one end, sloping down to a pool of water about two inches deep. Small stones or a piece of wood at the bottom edge of the soil will keep it from sliding down into the water. Add a piece of curved bark to serve as a hiding place, as these animals like to have a lot of privacy.

If you are keeping frogs, toads, or salamanders in your aqua-terrarium, you will need a lid or cover to prevent your pets from climbing or hopping out. This can be a tight-fitting wooden frame to which you've tacked some wire screening.

Using an aquarium tank as a true aquarium, you can learn much about certain other herpetological specimens,

tadpoles in particular. During early spring, many ponds are thick with amphibian eggs and tadpoles. Place some pond water and pond plants, including the green scum (algae), in the water along with your collection of tapioca-like amphibian eggs and tadpoles. The pond plants will provide microscopic food for your growing tadpoles. It is fun as well as interesting to watch the tadpoles hatch from eggs, and to see frogs or toads develop from the tadpoles.

4. Kinds of Herpetological Pets

a. The Common Garter Snake, *Thanmophis sirtalis*

Garter snakes are found in every state; in fact, they're the most widely distributed snakes in North America (they're also found in the southern provinces of Canada). These snakes are extremely secretive, remaining hidden much of the time, but they are liable to turn up almost anywhere. When first handled they will usually bite (harmlessly) and secrete musk, but they will calm down in captivity. They are often found in gardens or on grassy lawns, where they feed on earthworms and small toads, and are also common along brooks and streams, where they catch

113

small frogs for food. They are particularly interesting because they are live bearing—giving birth to fully formed young—and also because of the size of their brood —there may be twenty to sixty young born at a time. You should feed your garter snake earthworms, small frogs, and toads, or even small fish.

b. The Hog-nosed Snake (genus *Heterodon*)

Easy to keep as a pet; interesting because it likes to pretend to be ferocious when it is actually almost completely harmless, and interesting also because it often plays dead. Sometimes it will roll on its back after writhing as though it were in great pain, and will then lie completely still, with its tongue in the dust, "playing dead." It will coil and even strike when it is molested, but it never bites. However, it will sometimes try to swallow fingers that have handled toads. As it is a rear-fanged snake, it cannot imbed its fangs by striking, but *can* do so when attempting to swallow a finger, causing a venomous reaction. Therefore it is to be handled with a little extra care. Your pet hog-nosed snake should be fed small frogs or toads.

c. Eastern King Snake (*Lampropeltis getulus getulus*)

King snakes make excellent pets, and will live in captivity for years. A king snake's cage should be kept clean and dry, with a pan of water and a place to hide as part of its furniture. You may feed king snakes frogs, toads, mice, and other snakes. In fact, it is immune to snake venom, even that of rattlesnakes, and is called "king snake" because of its habit of eating other snakes.

d. American Toad (*Bufo americanus americanus*)

The melodious trill of this little amphibian after the first showers in April is a welcome sound of spring. Toads spend the winter underground, not necessarily near water. After emerging from hibernation they make their way to the nearest pond or creek. Toads eat great quantities of insects. They can be fed mealworms, but the brown cricket sold commercially for fish bait is an even better food for frogs and toads. Toads, in spite of the popular tradition, never cause warts. Glands behind their eyes do secrete a substance that is distasteful, even poisonous, to dogs or wolves or other predators, but that is not dangerous to humans. If you do not wash your hands after handling *Bufo,* however, you could have a painful reaction in your eyes or a bad taste in your mouth if you put your hands absentmindedly to your face. The *Bufo marinus* of the lower Rio Grande Valley is particularly likely to have a harmful effect if not handled properly. It should be remembered, however, that, because of their destruction of great numbers of insect pests, toads are very valuable to man.

e. Frogs: Pickerel Frog, Wood Frog, Bullfrog, Northern Leopard Frog, Green Frog

Frogs are easy to catch in the springtime, and may be caught at night with a flashlight, as previously mentioned. They become so intent upon singing, apparently, that light doesn't bother them. Frogs must have a moist cage or aqua-terrarium. Bullfrogs will sit for hours in water up to their eyes. They may be fed mealworms, brown crickets, or earth-worms, and will often eat small pieces of raw beef. But they take only moving food, so bits of beef must be placed on a straw or string and moved about at feeding time.

f. Spotted Salamander (*Ambystoma maculatum*); Tiger Sal-amander (*Ambystoma tigrinum*)

Salamanders may be found under rocks or logs, in moist places. They make good pets, and should be fed mealworms and other insects. Keep salamanders in moist aqua-ter-rariums, and in a cool place. Some species live out their lives in cool dark caves. The western forms of the tiger salamander reproduce while still in the gill stage—they are called "neotenic." The cause of this appears to be insuffi-cient iodine in the diet.

g. Mud Puppy (*Necturus maculosus*)

Close relatives of salamanders, mud puppies keep their larval gills throughout their adult lives. They live in per-manent streams and lakes over most of the United States. They may be kept as pets, but their living conditions are demanding. For a full-grown mud puppy, you really should have a large tank, preferably a fifty-gallon one; and the water should be aerated with an aquarium pump. The temperature must be cool—not over 70°. Mud puppies will eat worms of all kinds, as well as crustaceans. In fact, they are such voracious feeders that they cannot be kept with smaller animals.

h. Gray Tree Frog (*Hyla versicolor*); Green Tree Frog (*Hyla cinereus*)

Tree frogs make interesting pets because of their acrobatic performances, and their ability to change color. They will wander over the sidewalls of their aqua-terrarium with ease, pressing their sticky toe-discs against the glass. Their body colors are green, gray, or brown, and vary according to light and temperature. It will take a tree frog an hour or two to change from green to brown under some conditions, although the change is sometimes much faster, a difference that may depend upon light and temperature. The call of the green tree frog is a surprise to all who hear it for the first time—more like the quack of a duck than the typical trill of a frog or toad. The grey tree frog has a more usual soft musical trill four to ten seconds in duration. Their cage should be kept quite damp, or your tree frogs will not live. Allow some plants to grow in their cage, too.

i. Horned Toads (properly called Horned Lizards (*Phrynosoma cornutum* is the Texas variety)

These lizards with toad-like shapes live in sandy places, burying their flattened bodies in the sand by sidewise movements. Unfortunately, in the northeast they seldom survive for long outside zoos, the difficulty of providing a high temperature and proper food in winter being a limiting factor. They live mostly on ants, but may be fed on mealworms and other live and moving insects. As captives, they need a few inches of dry sand and several hours of

sunlight daily. The temperature should always be at least 70°. They will eat only when warm, and will go for weeks without food. These animals illustrate protective coloration to a remarkable extent, their body markings making them obscure no matter what background they are placed against. A dozen different kinds of horned lizards live in the western half of the United States. Occasionally these lizards squirt jets of blood from the corners of their eyes, but they seldom perform the feat in captivity.

j. The American Anole, or Chameleon (*Anolis carolinensis*).

Anoles may change back and forth from various browns and greens to suit their surroundings, or due to excitement. When winning a fight they are a brilliant green; when asleep they are pale green. When losing a fight, or when lying in the sun, they turn a deep brown. A change in color requires two or three minutes. Anoles can also roll their eyes independently of one another. When excited, the male anole often extends a pink or red throat fan. These lizards, distantly related to the horned lizards, may be bought at pet shops, at state fairs, and at circuses. They must be kept at a temperature of about 85°. The easiest of all lizards to keep, they should be housed in an aqua-terrarium with plenty of moisture and a glass cover, which should be removed once a day to admit fresh air. Don't pick an anole (or any other Iguanid lizard) up by its tail, for the tail will break off! A new tail will grow, but often shorter than the original one and always with a different scale pattern. Anoles eat living insects, but the insects must be moving or they will be refused. Anoles crawl over glass as do tree frogs, for they have similar adhesive plates under their toes.

k. Fence Lizard or Pine Tree Lizard (*Sceloporus undulatus*)

These fast-moving lizards are fairly common from the Atlantic coast to Arizona and Utah. They are hard to catch because of their speed. They have large scales and are sometimes called scaly lizards. Look for them in pine groves or forests. Male fence lizards have blue patches on the under-side and are sometimes accused (wrongly) of being poison-ous. They are usually about five or six inches long, are suita-ble for a small terrarium, and must be fed live insects.

l. Five-lined Skink (*Eumeces fasciatus*)

Usually found on the ground, skinks are active during the day, but are very secretive. In the South they are called scorpions. Smooth and glossy, they live in moist places, usu-ally in the woods. The young are blue tailed, and are called "blue-tailed skinks" as though they were another species. Large adult males lose the dark and light stripes, and in breeding season may turn a reddish color. Usually found under large decaying logs, or under bark slabs in the vicin-ity of a sawmill, they will try to bite, but their bite is harmless because their teeth are small. Skinks are easily kept in captivity; they may be fed small pieces of raw meat and a variety of insects, and have been known to eat small amounts of raw egg.

m. Gopher Tortoise (*Gopherus polyphemus*—Florida species)

Known in the south as "gophers," these turtles are easily kept in cages. Another species is found in extreme south Texas, and a third in Arizona. All are in danger of extinc-tion, and should they lay eggs in captivity the event might offer a good opportunity to contact a nearby zoo or museum of natural history for advice on the care of the eggs. These tortoises should be kept in a warm and very dry terrarium. If their cage is moist, they will probably die. Often found in sandy areas, they burrow underground, and have been known to dig down for twenty feet below the surface. They will live in the same burrows for years. Like other tortoises, these animals live to a ripe old age, sometimes reaching one hundred years. When they are old, their shells are smooth, but when young the shields on the carapace have a pattern of concentric grooves. Gopher tortoises are largely vege-tarian—eating berries and small pieces of fruit, celery, let-tuce, and even grass. They grow to a foot or more in length, and may weigh nine or ten pounds. Handle them carefully, or they will scratch with their sharp claws.

n. Cumberland Terrapin or Slider (*Pseudemys scripta*)

These terrapins are called sliders because of their habit of sliding into the water when disturbed. In the midwest and southwest they are called the red-eared turtle. They are the best sellers in pet shops. Many thousands are sold every year over most of the United States. In the southern United States, they are the most abundant of turtles. Beautifully colored, they have a green shell, scarlet bands on each side of the head, and greatly varied markings on the undersides of their shells. No two are ever marked alike. They should be placed in an aqua-terrarium, as they require both land and water. They prefer temperatures of between 75° and 80°. Their favorite foods are earthworms, tiny pieces of fish, and chopped raw meat, to which you should add cod-liver oil from time to time. Commercial turtle food is not recommended for these or any other turtles. Although usually two or three inches long in pet shops, they may grow to twelve inches or more.

o. The Box Turtle (*Terrapene carolina*)

Box turtles, with their dome-shaped shells and bright orange or yellow markings, are attractive and make good pets. They are harmless to handle and easily confined; and they will eat a great variety of food, including mushrooms, snails, caterpillars, berries, melon, lettuce, bananas, bread, and mealworms. Furthermore, they'll go for weeks without any food. But they should always be supplied with water. Primarily land dwellers, they are usually found in woods along streams. Females lay their eggs in June or July, in a flask-shaped cavity in soft soil. The eggs hatch in September or October, and the young turtles soon hibernate for the winter.

5. *Your Herpetological Notebook and Reference File*

Get yourself a sturdy notebook, one of the hardback composition notebooks available in dime stores for about thirty-five cents. Number the pages at the top or bottom, and begin to make notes on your captive specimens, or your field observations, always recording the date of entry. Make detailed notes on the actions or events in the lives of any reptiles or amphibians you are able to see and study.

Buy yourself a pack of 3" x 5" cards and a box with a file index, and begin a card reference file. Make a card for each herpetological book or publication that is relevant to your interests. First write down the author's name, then the title of the book or bulletin or magazine article. Go to your library and look through the card catalogue for titles that may be of special interest, and note them for your own reference file. Then begin a program of reading or examining these books and other publications. You will be following a procedure used by professionals, and thus will teach yourself to be a good amateur naturalist. Keep your reading notes in a separate notebook, perferably a loose-leaf one, write on one side of the page only, and give each page a heading, or "slug."

6. Your Herpetological Scrapbook

Start a scrapbook of clippings, magazine articles, photographs, drawings, cartoons, anything on reptiles and amphibians. Watch the papers and magazines for suitable material for your scrapbook. Until you have time to mount them in the scrapbook, you can file your clippings and tear sheets in a big brown envelope.

7. Build and Keep a Vivarium Habitat

An ideal way to observe and at the same time control your reptiles and amphibians is to keep them in a vivarium habitat display case. This project must be limited, however, to the smaller kinds of specimens, such as young turtles, salamanders, and lizards. Obtain a small or medium-sized aquarium and arrange soil, damp mosses, and small woodland plants, including ferns, in it. Cover the top with a sheet of glass, held a little above the rim by matchsticks so that air may circulate while the plants remain damp, keeping your salamanders or other small specimens alive. You may feed your stock on termites, ants, mealworms, or small pieces of earthworms, remembering that as a rule these amphibians must see their prey moving before they will feed. Keep a notebook on everything that you see happening in your vivarium; at any time you may observe something new that will be of value to naturalists.

8. Preserved Specimens for Your Home Museum

In order to learn more about herpetology, you will want to make a collection of preserved specimens for your home museum. It is better not to go out into the field to collect specimens for preservation: some reptiles and amphibians are quite rare, and only the expert scientist should develop a preserved collection from the field. But many of the reptiles and amphibians which you keep in your vivarium or reptile zoo will have short lives regardless of the good care they may receive. When one of your live specimens dies you will have your chance to begin a preserved collection. Take your dead reptile or amphibian without delay and cut a small slit in its belly. Wash the specimen under the tap until no more blood appears. Next, drop the specimen into diluted rubbing alcohol. You can obtain the rubbing alcohol (a chemical that is harmless to the skin and gives off no irritating fumes) at any drugstore; to dilute it properly, mix it with an equal amount of water. In four or five days, transfer the specimen to *undiluted* rubbing alcohol for permanent preservation in a glass jar with a screw top. The neatest way to show the specimen off is to arrange and tie it onto a glass slide or plate before inserting it into the jar. Be sure to make a label on a white index card, giving both the common and technical (Latin) name of the specimen, together with the date and locality where it was collected, and fasten the card to the top of the jar. You can also make a smaller label and tie it to the bottom of the mounting plate to be inserted into the solution with the specimen, but in that case you should print the label in India ink, which will not run or fade in rubbing alcohol. To prepare a really good-looking label, type it out first, properly spaced, and then ink over these typewritten letters with the India ink.

9. Photography of Reptiles

Photographs of reptiles can be made both in nature and under controlled conditions. You should be able to get some fine pictures on field trips, but even more detailed ones can be made inside. One of the best ways in which to control your reptiles is to put them into the refrigerator for a short time. This will make them sluggish, and they will allow themselves to be placed in any position in which you want to photograph them.

Bibliography

Your Guide to Further Reading

You should begin your further reading on reptiles and amphibians by consulting whatever encyclopedias are available, at home, at school, or in your library. Read the main articles under "reptiles" and "amphibians," and then look up "snakes," "frogs," "turtles," et cetera. When the titles of books are given, jot these down for further study.

There are many excellent books on reptiles and amphibians that you may either buy or borrow from your library. There are also many helpful and inexpensive museum bulletins and leaflets on herpetology. One of these that should prove especially useful is *Reptiles and Amphibians of the Northeastern States,* by Roger Conant, 3rd edition 1957, Zoological Society of Philadelphia, Philadelphia. It is available from the publisher, the Philadelphia Zoological Society.

A list of books follows:

a. *Living Reptiles of the World,* by Karl P. Schmidt and Robert F. Inger, 1957, Hanover House, Garden City. N. Y.

b. *Living Amphibians of the World,* by Doris M. Cochran, 1961, Hanover House, Garden City, N. Y.

These two books are exceptional. They are filled with photographs, both in black and white and in color, the latter of which are the finest color photographs of herpetological specimens that have ever been published. Exceedingly interesting and fully authoritative, these two books could well serve as your basic herpetological texts for years to come.

c. *Snakes Alive and How They Live,* by Clifford Pope, 1937, N. Y. Viking Press.
This is one of the most fascinating introductions to the natural history of snakes.

d. *The Natural History of North American Amphibians and Reptiles,* by James A. Oliver, 1955, D. Van Nostrand Co., Inc., Princeton.
This is an excellent study of the general biology of these animals.

e. *A Field Guide to Reptiles and Amphibians of Eastern North America,* by Roger Conant, 1958, Houghton Mifflin Company, Boston.

f. *Amphibians and Reptiles of Western North America,* by Robert C. Stebbins, 1954, McGraw-Hill Book Co., Inc.

g. *Introduction to Herpetology,* by C. J. Goin and O. B. Goin, 1962, W. H. Freeman & Co., San Francisco.

h. *Dictionary of Herpetology,* by James A. Peters, 1964, Hafner Publishing Co., Inc., New York.

Finally, it should be repeated that interested students of reptiles and amphibians should make an effort to become acquainted with an active herpetologist. Such individuals may be found on the faculty of a college or university, or on the staff of a natural history museum. Many cities now have youth museums or natural science centers where young people interested in natural science can receive special attention. In addition, joining one of the national societies, such as The American Society of Ichthyologists and Herpetologists, or the Herpetological League, is recommended to any student with serious interests in this branch of natural science. Such students would find it helpful to obtain a copy of *Career Opportunities For the Herpetologist,* a free bulletin that may be had by writing to The American Society of Ichthyologists and Herpetologists, U. S. National Museum, Washington, D. C. 20560.

A List of the Books and Popular Writings of Karl Patterson Schmidt.

GROUP 1. MUSEUM BOOKLETS AND SPECIAL PUBLICATIONS

1. *The American Alligator,* 1922, Zoology Leaflet No. 3, Field Museum of Natural History.
2. *The Truth About Snake Stories,* 1929, Zoology Leaflet No. 10, Field Museum of Natural History.
3. *The Frogs and Toads of the Chicago Area,* 1929, Zoology Leaflet No. 11, Chicago (Field Museum).
4. *The Salamanders of the Chicago Area,* 1930, Zoology Leaflet No. 12, Field Museum of Natural History.
5. *Amphibians and Reptiles of the Chicago Region,* 1935, with Walter L. Necker, Bulletin No. 5, Chicago Academy of Sciences.
6. *Turtles of the Chicago Area,* 1938, Zoology Leaflet No. 14, Field Museum of Natural History.
7. *Crocodile-hunting in Central America,* Popular Series No. 15, 1952, Chicago Natural History Museum.
8. "Herpetology," in *A Century of Progress in the Natural Sciences,* 1955, California Academy of Sciences.
9. "Animal Geography," in *A Century of Progress in the Natural Sciences,* 1955, California Academy of Sciences.

GROUP 2. BOOKS

1. *Homes and Habits of Wild Animals,* 1934, M. A. Donohue Co., N. Y.
2. *Ecological Animal Geography,* 1937, with W. C. Alee, John Wiley & Sons, N. Y. An authorized rewritten edition based on Richard Hesse's *Ecological Foundations of Animal Geography.*
3. *Our Friendly Animals and Whence They Came,* 1938, M. A. Donohue Company, N. Y. Re-issued in 1947 under title *Our Friendly Animals.*
4. *Field Book of Snakes of the United States and Canada,* 1941, with D. Dwight Davis, G. P. Putnam's Sons, New York.
5. *Principles of Animal Ecology,* 1949, with W. C. Allee, Alfred E. Emerson, Orlando Park, Thomas Park, W. B. Saunders Company.
6. *A Check List of North American Amphibians and Reptiles,* 1953, 6th edition, Univ. of Chicago Press.

126

7. *Living Reptiles of the World*, 1957, with Robert F. Ingar, Doubleday and Company, Inc., Garden City. N. Y.

GROUP 3. ARTICLES PUBLISHED IN MAGAZINES AND MUSEUM JOURNALS

1. "Robert Kennicott, Founder of Museums," *The Chicago Naturalist*, 1936, Vol. 7, No. 1.
2. "Tall Tales About Snakes," 1938, *Science Digest*, April, 1938.
3. "The Guano Islands of Peru," *Chicago Naturalist*, 1940, Vol. 3, No. 1.
4. "A Cloud Forest Camp in Honduras," *The Chicago Naturalist*, 1942, Vol. 5, No. 1.
5. "What is a Naturalist? (A Study in Natural History)," *The Chicago Naturalist*, 1943, Vol. 6.
6. "Crocodiles," *Fauna*, 1944, Vol. 6.
7. "The Paraguayan Pantanal," 1946, *The Chicago Naturalist*.
8. "The Hoop Snake Story," *Natural History Magazine*, 1925, Vol. 25.
9. "A Naturalist's Glimpse of the Andes," *Scientific Monthly*, 1945, Vol. 60.
10. "The Sierra del Carmen in Northern Coahuila," *Texas Geographic Magazine*, 1946.
11. "How to Make Money Frog Farming," *Turtox News*, 1946, Vol. 24.
12. "Chastine Revisited," *The Chicago Naturalist*, 1947, Vol. 10, No. 1.